BEFORE YOU MARRY

Daniel G. Bagby & Michael M. Massar

Convention Press
Nashville, Tennessee

Contents

The Writers 4

Introduction 5

Chapter 1 Why Should I Marry? 6

Chapter 2 What Do I Expect of Marriage? 22

Chapter 3 How Do I Communicate? 40

Chapter 4 What Do I Believe and Live By? 52

Chapter 5 What Kind of Manager Am I? 66

Chapter 6 How Do I Express My Sexuality? 82

Chapter 7 What Am I to Do? And You? 94

Chapter 8 What Is My Family Like?
 What Will My New Family Be? 108

Group Learning Activities 121

The Church Study Course 143

Church Study Course Form 144

*T*he Writers

Daniel G. Bagby, writer of chapters 1-3, 5-6, and 8, was born in Porto Alegre, Brazil, where his parents were missionaries. His grandparents were the first Southern Baptist missionaries to Brazil.

Dan is a graduate of The Southern Baptist Theological Seminary in Louisville, Kentucky, where he received training in theology, psychology, and pastoral care.

As pastor of Seventh and James Baptist Church in Waco, Texas, Dan spends considerable time counseling and leading family life and marriage enrichment seminars. Contacts with youth and young adults occur frequently, since his church is adjacent to the campus of Baylor University.

Dan and his wife, Janet, are the parents of two children, Douglas and Bryn.

Michael M. Masser, writer of chapters 4 and 7 and the personal and group learning activities, is pastor of First Baptist Church, Clemson, South Carolina. Previously, he served as pastor of Wildewood Baptist Church, Houston, Texas.

A graduate of Baylor University, Southwestern Baptist Theological Seminary, and Graduate Theological Foundation at Notre Dame, Mike has had extensive experience in leading family life seminars and retreats. His hobbies include reading, writing, and golf.

Mike and his wife, Lisa, are the parents of Matthew, Patrick, and Meredith.

*I*ntroduction

Many people grow up believing that they will marry. Some never question whether they should marry. Few stop to consider what marriage is all about. This book is designed as a guide for making decisions about marriage now and in the future.

Numerous books have been designed for persons who are already planning to get married and are now preparing for that commitment. The main emphasis of this study is to help you determine the role and function of marriage from a Christian viewpoint and to help you discover what questions and issues you need to raise when contemplating marriage.

Each chapter opens with a question about an issue related to marriage—God's purpose for marriage, expectations and options, communication, beliefs to live by, managing finances, expressing sexuality, vocation, in-law relationships. Periodically, you will be challenged to STOP AND THINK and express your opinions about the concepts that have been presented.

Sharing hopes and dreams is a part of preparation for marriage.

WHY SHOULD I MARRY?

*T*he first chapter of Genesis informs us that God made male and female in His own image (v. 27). The second chapter of Genesis emphasizes that God made them for each other (v. 18). The first four chapters of Genesis reveal the spirit and atmosphere in which this human partnership was formed. What were the main characteristics of the partnership? What was God's purpose for the partnership? STOP AND THINK! Write your ideas in the following exercise.

Stop and Think 1

What do you think is the purpose for marriage? Record your thoughts.

_____

_____

Qualities of Relationships

The God of creation has placed within us the need for community. We were designed to live in communities as families. Considering this fact, three key qualities seem to describe marriage relationships. They are *dependence, responsibility, and fidelity*.

Dependence

Jean wasn't quite sure why she was uncomfortable around Tim. They had been dating for several months, but she still felt "tied up" around him most of the time. Her feelings worried her. She cared for Tim a lot; but, at the same time, she resented him. Then one day, as she was talking to her mother, her father came up and asked her opinion about weekend plans. Suddenly it hit her: Tim never asked her opinion about anything! She knew she didn't know everything, but she was getting tired of always doing what Tim wanted to do. Did liking him mean she always had to do what he wanted?

Marriage is a commitment involving two persons who choose to be deeply dependent on each other.

We came into this world as dependent creatures. Our development and growth are movements toward independence. Young people, living by God's design, become more and more self-sufficient. Our identity as individuals is not complete until we move away from parents and decide who we will be on our own. Such a process makes us independent for the first time. From that way of living we have the option to choose again—to become dependent on someone else.

In the maturing days of youth, we arrive at a point in life when we begin to choose voluntarily to become dependent. We do so first with chosen friends. We involve ourselves in relationships with the opposite sex and carefully choose how dependent we will become. Then comes the decision about marriage.

Marriage is a chosen act—a process involving a person's will and desire. In the cautious, careful choosing of a mate, we take on the voluntary process of becoming dependent on another person. This choice is a deliberate placing of oneself in a partnership relationship. In the King James Version, the biblical words describe woman's relationship with man as "an help meet for him" (Gen. 2:18). The words *help meet* translate as one "fit" for another, a friend and companion, who is an equal, placed alongside to assist, to complement.

One of God's purposes in making two different kinds of human beings was to help us see how we need other people. Our human make up and feelings enable us to understand our dependence. The One who created us designed us to depend on others. Marriage is a commitment involving two persons who choose to be deeply dependent on each other.

When we consider marriage we should think about dependence. If we have just spent much time and energy becoming independent, we may not want to share decisions and choices with someone else. We may need more time to enjoy our new-found freedom. We need to figure out whether we want to depend on another human being for life.

Stop and Think 2

Do you think everyone should get married?

_____ Yes _____ No

Complete the chart by listing the main advantage and disadvantage of the married and single life-styles.

	Being Single	Being Married
Advantage	_____	_____
Disadvantage	_____	_____

One indication that a person is becoming an adult appears when the individual is able to look beyond self. When a person begins to consider another's feelings as much as his or her own, that individual demonstrates a capacity to reach out, a willingness to become dependent. Choosing to depend is an important step in preparation for marriage.

The dependence experienced by adults in a marriage relationship is a *mutual* dependence, sometimes called interdependence. That is, each person depends on the other as much as he or she is depended on. That kind of depending is balanced and healthy and stimulates growth. The word *inter* simply means "between two" and refers to the ability to exchange need and care. Good marriages involve mutual dependence.

Responsibility

Jim hesitated for a moment before turning into the driveway. His hands perspired as he rang the doorbell. Ann answered. He swallowed hard and made his speech: "This is the third time you've left town without telling me when and where you were going. I've been worried sick not knowing where you were and how you were doing. I've just come from the bus station and have met every bus from Houston since noon. You told me to meet you there—on your only postcard—and then you changed your plans. I can't handle it anymore, Ann."

Ann shrugged her shoulders, smiled at Jim's concern, and replied: "Jim, you know I need freedom to be myself. If you have to know where I am and what I'm doing all the time, then we'll never get along. What are you trying to do—be my keeper?"

Marriage does not mean taking responsibility away from each person in the relationship; rather, it involves accepting a new, mutual responsibility. One who considers caring for another in marriage also chooses to become responsible. Marriage partners not only accept responsibility for themselves, they also assume responsibility for the relationship.

What is involved is a conscious decision to accept the care and sustaining of another individual. Persons who examine marriage need to think carefully about this decision.

Those who marry are to assume the challenge of helping their chosen partner develop in all phases of life. They encourage the potential of their mate. They offer support and agree to care for and help that person achieve goals in life. Such a commitment is not to be taken quickly or lightly—just as the traditional marriage ceremony states: "Not unadvisedly, . . . but discreetly, . . . in the fear of God."

Caring for another person is a decision of the will. We decide to commit ourselves to someone else—to the point of assuming responsibility. We do not interfere in the individual's need to be responsible for herself; we become responsible alongside the person. God is the model of such responsibility; for He takes on the obligation of caring for us without taking away our responsibility for ourselves.

Marriage involves accepting a new, mutual responsibility.

A significant issue to a Christian who is considering marriage is whether or not the person is prepared to assume responsibility for someone else. Marriage, from the first pages of Genesis on through the Bible, is defined as a call to responsibility.

Fidelity

She drew her head back, wiped the tears from her eyes, and continued the letter: "No matter how many times I tell myself that I can trust you and that it doesn't matter when I see you out with someone else, I can't live with that feeling. Try as I may, Ralph, I still want to believe that someone who tells me he is 'ready to settle down' really wants to stick by me. I can't live wondering every day if you are going to be there for me—if you still need to look around and share your interest in many people. I'm not there anymore, Ralph. I want someone who is going to be there tomorrow—for me—in a way he's not there for anyone else. Is that asking too much? Does trust mean the other person can do what he pleases, or does it grow from knowing the other person will always be there for you?"

The issue of fidelity (loyalty) is central to all relationships. God defines His covenant with human beings on the basis of such allegiance. We live out God's design for our relationship with Him as we develop the ability to become faithful to another person.

We use the word *loyalty* to describe a chosen devotion and commitment that involves the capacity to "stick by" people and principles. In the youth years, we experience this commitment through loyalty to peers. We develop the quality of fidelity by learning to devote ourselves consistently to one person.

At the center of love and marriage, from a biblical perspective, is the capacity to trust and be trusted. Marriages governed by Christian principles are unique because they are characterized by the trait of fidelity. The Christian perspective assumes loyalty on a continuous basis. That is why mature relationships are not measured on how a person feels but on what a person has willed. Relationships and commitments based on will are far more enduring than those based on feelings alone. They are determined by a rational decision to stand by choices and promises. The cultivation and growth of fidelity in a relationship are crucial to Christian marriage.

Stop and Think 3

Define *fidelity*.

_____

Explain why this quality is absolutely essential in marriage.

_____

_____

Relationships Reflecting God

When God created male and female, He endowed them with basic characteristics of Himself. How do we reflect the nature and personality of our Maker?

Parenting

David looked slowly away from the window and into Gretchen's eyes. For the first time what he was about to say didn't scare him! He suddenly realized that his fear of having a child was the fear that he was not wanted when he was a baby and that he could not be a good father. His voice trembled as he said: "If—if you are ready to have a baby and if you don't mind the mistakes I'll make and if you promise that a girl will look just like you, then I guess I'm ready to be a dad."

Gretchen had waited seven long years to see David's face when he might say that. She walked over to him, and they both embraced and cried. Their tears were not a simple bond—they cried in fear, relief, and joy.

God shared a "maximum" gift in the creation of human beings. He could have invented many different ways for us to reproduce ourselves. The rest of His creation proves that. The Lord of life, however, chose to make the creative act one that is based on all His nature. He took a man and a woman; brought them to a growing understanding of care, fidelity, dependence, responsibility, and trust; and, with all these ingredients, created the capacity to love. God made man and woman in such a way that, in the privacy and intimacy of a committed relationship, we could offer ourselves to each other. The human experience of "knowing," as the Bible describes the sexual encounter, is the full revealing and receiving of each other. This experience is not just physical; it also involves spiritual, physical, and mental communion.

God so ordained human bodies that, in the full expression of love, two people could join together to create another human being in the image of their love. From the union of two loving persons there emerges a child, shaped in the image of the couple's love! In this creation God shares with humanity one of the most beautiful truths of life: Out of love, He made us in His own image.

Such incredible truth explains why Christians should reserve full sexual intimacy for marriage. We believe a relationship that cultivates care, mutual dependence, responsibility, fidelity, and commitment provides the proper setting for the expression of sexual love. Here the biblical explanation of "one flesh" is etablished. Two persons, carefully choosing each other, develop the trust and faithfulness required to share in oneness. They thus express the harmonious meshing of two individuals. A new identity is formed. They don't lose their individuality; they share together unity of purpose under God.

The gift of life in children allows a couple to share not only in creating but also in the joy of parenting. God, the Father of all, thus shares the function of parenting. He is a father who nurtures, sustains, develops, and guides each of His children. The calling of parenthood involves an ongoing responsibility and faithfulness.

From time to time, people considering marriage talk about having children. Some understand the joy and responsibility that is combined in such a task. Others are surprised later when being a parent is not always fun. Anyone considering marriage needs to evaluate the gift of parenting. This is an experience that calls for patience, joy, faithfulness to a long-term goal, and commitment to another life. Not all young people are prepared to accept such responsibilities.

Fellowship

John sat across from the counselor's table, confused and angry. "I've given her the best home possible, no responsibility for working, three fine children, and the best set of friends in town. Why can't she be happy?"

"Because," Ginny replied, "I don't have you anymore, John. When we started off, we had a little house, no children, and few friends—but I had you. We shared our moments, all of them. Now you're so busy getting me everything you think I need that you're not around to give me the most important thing I want—you!"

One of the frequently misunderstood passages in the Old Testament is God's command to "be fruitful and multiply" (Gen. 1:28). Most explanations of this Scripture refer to God's desire that the earth be supplied with inhabitants in the early days of humanity. While that interpretation is valid, the meaning is broader. The context (the place and situation in which a comment is stated) sheds information about the deeper meaning of this instruction.

Both comments about being fruitful follow the explanation that we have been created in God's image. God was saying that He intended for His creation to be fruitful and multiply in keeping with His image—His nature and way. What does that mean? Basically it means that God was far less concerned with multiplying numbers of people and far more concerned with creating the fellowship and communion for which He made humans.

The biblical idea of marriage brings out the best in human experience.

Those who follow God's purpose are to multiply the spirit and attitude of the Father. Such a purpose means we have been designed for fellowship with God and with one another. The deep bonds of care and love that develop between us are part of God's hope in creating. God knows that the creating of human beings with the right attitude and desire increases the belonging and fellowship for which we all yearn. The more that atmosphere of care and belonging is multiplied, the more we follow His purposes for us and for Himself.

Thus, God is not interested in creating only for the sake of creating. He wants people to be related to one another and to assume care, interest, and kinship among themselves. He knows the value of fellowship for support. He understands the meaning of shared ties. He produces families for the purpose of fellowship. He shapes communities to provide the care, mutual dependence, and support that is necessary. God's image in us is by nature a desire for fellowship. As we follow His image in us, we reflect His purpose of fellowship: that all His creations may be related in care and harmony.

Love

He sat in stunned silence, overcome with resentment because of Deborah's words. She looked him straight in the eye and confessed that she had been unfaithful to him. What now? What was she waiting for? What was there left to say? The silence was heavy. She stared at him, then down to the floor.

He cleared his throat and said softly, "I still love you, Debbie."

"What does that mean?" She trembled back.

"It means," he said with a burdened sigh, "that I don't want to quit."

Her eyes were full; she did not understand—and yet, she was relieved.

God's image in creation is reflected not only in the desire for fellowship, but also in the multiplying of love. The second mandate in humanity's mission in Genesis was to generate love. The multiplying of love is at the core of who God is. Those, therefore, who are made in His image, are called to multiply His love.

Marriage is the sustaining structure for both fellowship and love. The reproducing of God's image in communion and love is a central function of marriage. Those who commit themselves to the biblical view of marriage hold a high calling. They are devoted to the increase and multiplication of God's love! As already emphasized, such love is based on a voluntary investment of oneself in another person. This love is sustained by a faithfulness to a particular relationship and is continuing and steady. The love that God wants multiplied is grounded in His image and, as such, is founded on an attitude of mutual development and fulfillment.

The best possible human exchange for "reproducing" the communion and love of God is the marriage setting. That is why Christians so often become committed to marriage. The biblical idea of marriage brings out the best in human experience.

===== **Stop and Think 4** =====

Read 1 Corinthians 13:4-7. Write your definition of love based on these verses and the discussion in this section.

Love is _____

Vulnerability

"Why? Why is the pain so cruel? Why can't I just walk away like he did a moment ago and let what happened slip into the past? Why do I need to hurt, Lord? God, it hurts so much! Is there no other way to care?"

And then she heard a quiet voice inside her say: "No. There is no other way—to place your life into someone else's life—deep care, deep hurt. I wouldn't want the love to be shallow."

By now, you should have a clearer picture of God's intent for marriage. All of the characteristics described in this chapter are shaped by a central attitude: Adequate care, interdependence, responsibility, and fidelity are not possible without vulnerability—the willingness to open oneself to another person.

The idea of being "vulnerable" is made clear in the biblical message about God. He chose to reveal Himself to human beings. He did not have to do so; but His commitment of love means that He opens His life and nature to us. He becomes vulnerable because He chooses to be known. As He makes Himself known, God risks abuse, misunderstanding, and rejection. Still, He is willing to take that risk.

The fabric of human bonding is knit by openness and trust. The deepest relationships are developed only in an atmosphere of sharing and willingness to be known. However, when one allows another person to know him or her openly, a risk is taken. Part of the risk of revelation is that, when people know us, they can misuse, misunderstand, or reject us. Vulnerability thus means that anyone who shares a deep relationship is open to hurt. We may be hurt by those who use knowledge and understanding about us as weapons against us. We may be misunderstood by others who are so caught up in their own needs that they misuse us. We can be rejected because, when people come to know us as we are, they may not like what they know.

The risk of knowing also is a burden. Any individual who has had another person share deeply and personally knows the responsibility of trust. Such a gift involves the weight of knowing and the vulnerability that these revelations bring. Sharing deeply with someone is to give and to forgive.

The deepest relationships are developed in an atmosphere of sharing.

=== **Stop and Think 5** ===

Talk to a married friend that you feel has a happy marriage. Ask that person this question: What are some things you share with your mate? Write the person's responses here.

_____

_____

_____

Covenant

Marriage has a special biblical design. As noted already, its purposes date back to creation and to a God who designed male and female to develop their highest potential. Such potential and purposes have special characteristics. The combined result of all these issues makes for a unique contract between two marrying partners. This unusual contract is called a covenant.

The word *covenant* is a biblical term for a binding agreement between two parties. Although a covenant is similar to a modern-day "contract," it has a much stronger force to it. A covenant is a contract that is followed at a level deeper than simply complying with the minimum acceptable to fulfill an agreement. In a covenant, the spirit of the agreement must be honored.

What the Bible means is that those who enter a covenant relationship participate with all the enthusiasm they have. They go beyond the requirements of the agreement and seek to fulfill the intent of the promise. Participants in covenants bring a mutual dependence and a desire to fulfill another into the promise of a covenant.

Covenant makers also commit themselves to be fully responsible for the outcome of their contract. They assume a continuous faithfulness to what they have promised. Rather than seek a way out of the contract, they seek ways to enrich the bond they have made. Those who enter into covenants work to enhance the strength of their promises.

Marriage covenants are established for life. Covenant keepers wish to nurture the agreement established and also to better the person with whom they entered the contract. Because they are personally involved in the chosen promises, covenant people invest their honor, their integrity, and their life into the marriage contract or covenant.

The seriousness of marriage covenants may frighten some people. Yet, a basic truth is that the most important steps in life usually are both difficult and satisfying. The God who designs difficult contracts offers with them the best things in life. He enters such covenants with us, declaring that He chooses only the best. He invites us to do the same.

Stop and Think 6

List the most important purposes for marriage. Then compare your answers with what you wrote in Stop and Think 1.

a. _____

b. _____

c. _____

What have you read in this chapter that has changed a view you had about the purpose of marriage? Record that discovery.

_____

_____

WHAT DO I EXPECT OF MARRIAGE?

*O*ften, we hope certain things will happen; we dream and wish. Naturally, when our dreams do not come true, we are very disappointed. Many people who become discouraged about their marriage have expectations that did not "turn out." What happened? In some cases what they expected was a secret; nobody knew what they wanted. In other cases, what the people found and what they expected were two different things.

=========== **Stop and Think 7** ===========

What do you expect of marriage? Write your ideas:

_____

_____

_____

_____

False Expectations

When expectations do not match the reality, frustration sets in. Possibly, such a situation develops because expectations are unrealistic. So, what should we expect of marriage? Let's look first at what not to expect—false expectations. Then we will examine realistic expectations—those things we may expect to happen in marriage because marriage can provide them.

False Idea 1: Love Is Mainly Feeling

The word *love* is used for many different purposes. We grow up hearing about love mainly as something that persons *feel* toward one another. We use the word to talk about feelings that we have for people, things, and events. We even use the word *love* to describe superficial feelings and attitudes: "I just love your dress." "She just loves the way he talks." The following conversation about "love" took place in a girl's rest room in a local high school.

> "Did you see that new guy from the East Coast who just transferred into Mrs. Stanley's homeroom? Wow! I'm in love!—I mean, I walked out into the gym, and, up in the bleachers, there was this human vision! I melted right there on the spot. I'm in love, Sue!"
>
> "Can you believe it? Isn't it fantastic? The same thing happened to me last year. I was at a Valentine's Day party with Joe, and this guy came out of nowhere and started talking with me. I had never, I mean never, laid my eyes on him before; but by the time we finished the conversation, I was madly in love."

What these girls described certainly was an emotional experience. All of us probably have had the same type of experience at some time in our lives. The surge of feelings inside, the rapid pulse rate, the internal signals of excitement, and the attraction to a certain person all are normal aspects of a boy-girl meeting. These are genuine feelings. Love, however, is not the right word to describe them.

Persons who experience strong feelings toward another person enjoy some of the responses God intended for human beings to have. These feelings, however, are neither permanent nor the main ingredient in love, as some would have us believe. The romantic idea that people just "fall" in love is not true. Those words imply that love just happens, that we have no control over its occurrence. That is simply not the case.

Ideas about romantic love are fed by several popular myths. The notion that on some "enchanted evening" we will meet a "stranger" who will be our "prince" or "princess charming" is quite popular. (Note the fairy-tale words in that statement and compare them to the conversation in the gym rest room.) What is described is not authentic love but the appearance of intense and enjoyable feelings. As enjoyable as these impressions are, they are emotions of a moment and will soon disappear.

The romantic idea that people just "fall" in love is not true.

Some who have had strong feelings toward others believe they are "falling out of love" when the feelings begin to disappear. They have been taught that love is mainly a constant set of emotional "highs"; thus, they naturally conclude that, if the emotional peaks are gone, so is their love. What they have done, however, is confuse romantic notions and changing moods with love. Feelings come and go; genuine love remains.

False Idea 2: There Is Only One

People often talk about "Mr. Right" and the "one and only" in their lives. The idea that there is one correct person for each of us is an old tradition, and it has been strengthened in Christian circles by the decision to seek God's will in life. However, following God's will does not necessarily mean there is only one person in someone's life. Perhaps a better understanding of God's will and purpose may help at this point.

As Christians, we have made a commitment to follow God's will for our lives. We sometimes confuse the idea of following Him down "the narrow road" with the mistaken idea that His will is a narrow set of choices. The God of creation and abundant living is not a God of few choices. He never has been.

Following God's will, then, is not limited to seeking the one choice in life we may have if we are doing what He wants. Rather, it involves choosing carefully from a variety of options that are in keeping with His will and purposes. For example, a thoughtful study of the Bible tells us that God rarely calls an individual to one job or vocation. God's will in Moses' life involved at least four different occupations—one after another. Neither is God's will a one-time choice that is never repeated. Jonah and others in the Old Testament are reminders that God comes to His people several times with choices and challenges.

The same idea applies to the choice of a mate. God has so formed us that we are capable of relating to several potential mates in a responsible Christian manner. God places us in experiences and situations where we have the opportunity to know many different persons. He has so made us that we are capable of being responsibly involved with any one of several persons.

The idea of a "one and only" is a belief to be employed *after* marriage is established. The notion that there is only one and that we might miss the one and only if we are not careful is frightening and dull. The creative God of the Bible works His will like a theme in a symphony: many variations are available.

One additional misconception about the "one and only" needs to be mentioned. Underneath the idea of only one is a narrow interpretation of the religious belief of "predestination," suggesting that God has so designed life that we have only one choice. The impression naturally follows that, unless we find the particular person, we are outside God's purpose. Baptists firmly believe that we are given a free will and that we are asked to choose in all matters of faith. The God of freedom is a God who has prepared many ways for us to follow His purposes. He will not leave us without choices.

Judy walked into the room to find her younger sister crying. "What's the story, Marsha? I heard you on the phone, and you sounded like the world had come to an end."

Marsha raised her head slowly. "It did as far as I'm concerned," she moaned. "Buddy just told me we're through—after almost three years of going together. I know I'll never find another one like him. There'll never be anybody else."

Judy smiled to herself, careful not to let her sister see her amusement. She remembered feeling the same way—twice. "I'm sorry it's hurting you so much, Marsh," she said softly. "I know, because you remember—it's happened to me, too. You're right. There is no one else like Buddy for you; but that doesn't mean there won't be someone else you'll care for as strongly as you care for Buddy."

Marsha's eyes narrowed as she looked up in anger. "There won't be anybody else! Nobody will ever be like Buddy! And I don't want anyone else if he's not Buddy!"

If you have ever "broken up" with someone you cared for, you probably know how Marsha felt. You also know that other experiences follow. Marsha had the right to say there would never be another Buddy. (God only makes one of a kind!) Marsha had a choice, however, when she declared that she would not accept anyone else. If we choose not to accept anyone else, that does not mean God has no other relationship for us in which His will and purpose can occur.

Stop and Think 8

Do you think God has prepared one special person for you? Why or why not?

_____

_____

_____

_____

False Idea 3: Everyone Should Marry

The purpose of God in creating two different human beings is carried out well in the institution of marriage. The life-style and purposes of marriage, however, are not necessarily designed for everyone. Some people have vocational and personal skills that require a solitary life-style. While they relate to many persons as friends, their schedule and work do not permit the intense requirements of marriage. They are committed to special purposes that the covenant of marriage may hinder.

Several persons in the Bible are good models of the single life-style. Certain prophets followed a life-style that required a "solo" existence. Elijah, Jeremiah, and Amos are examples. They are joined in the New Testament by such notables as Jesus Christ and Paul. The fact that Mary and Martha were single allowed them time and opportunity to minister to Jesus Christ. Consider the advantages of a single life-style as you read the following conversation.

"Jean, your father and I have been talking; and we want to share a deep concern we have for you. You are twenty-eight, well-established in your career and have excellent friends who seem just right for you. We can't understand why you aren't getting serious about anyone. Is there something wrong with what your father and I taught you? Is there something wrong about marriage? We see so many of your male friends whom we think so much of— bright, sensible young men. You don't seem interested in them at all. I mean, you are interested, but you don't seem to be interested enough!"

"Oh, Mother, I was wondering when we were going to get around to this conversation. I figured that pretty soon you two would be wondering about me—as if there were something wrong. The truth of the matter is, and it's just plain that; I want to be a single person! I love what I am doing; I like to travel. I thoroughly enjoy my friends, but I don't want to share an entire life with one of them alone. I really like the way things are!"

Somewhere along the way in your personal discovery, one important issue for you to consider is the place of marriage in your future. Marriage is not for everyone. Is it for you? Consider the matter carefully. What you decide will affect the rest of your life.

Stop and Think 9

What are some valid reasons for choosing not to marry?

_____

_____

False Idea 4: Love Is All You Need

The key to this illusion is that love is not understood in its deepest sense. If we could explain the word *love* and add all the ingredients it needs, then this statement might be more acceptable. What many people mean when they say, "Love is all you need," is that "good feelings" are all that is required. We challenged that nonsense when discussing the fiction that "love is mainly feeling."

What some people try to make us think is that the warm, positive feelings of romantic moments are all we need in a relationship. The tragedy of such a claim is that many people marry with that illusion. They actually believe that temporary feelings will carry them through life. These impressions are reinforced with movies and books, most of which show young men and women marrying after brief experiences and emotional "highs."

Joe and Linda had just told her parents that they were in love and were leaving together. At seventeen, they both had a year of high school ahead. When Joe's father told him that he had neither the money nor the job to start a marriage, Joe became angry, packed his gear, and came by to pick up Linda. Her parents had been supportive of their feelings and were trying to get them to think about all the responsibilities marriage demands. For every argument they introduced, the couple responded with determination to do what they wanted. Finally, tired of resisting Linda's parents, Joe declared: "It's no use, Linda. They simply don't understand."

Turning to the caring but defeated parents, Joe said: "You see, Mr. and Mrs. Tripp, Linda and I love each other. We care so deeply for each other that nothing can keep us apart. You mean well, but you don't understand. Being apart is just too hard on us. We can't wait anymore. There is nothing you can think of that we can't handle; we love each other, and that's the most important thing in the world. You ought to know that." The young couple got up, gathered their belongings, and left.

Joe and Linda were married that afternoon by a justice of the peace. They rented a duplex, dropped out of school, and started working. Linda was expecting in five months. Joe left soon after the child was born. He didn't want any competition for his time with Linda. And the glamour of the first few weeks was gone.

Joe and Linda had good intentions. Their feelings were genuine, but they lacked an understanding of what keeps couples together. In addition to warm, positive feelings, love is a determination to offer the best. Love includes the wisdom to postpone good things when better things take a little longer.

False Idea 5: Everyone Knows What to Expect

Mark and Susan, married for six months, were having "adjustment" problems. She was becoming increasingly angry with him, but he could not understand the problem. Finally they sat down to discuss the growing resentment. Susan started off by telling Mark that she was sick and tired of preparing meals for him every day when he was never there to enjoy them. She went on to say that she resented his coming and going as he pleased without a moment's explanation to her.

Mark was visibly stunned by Susan's comments. At first he was angry that she had confronted him. After a short conversation with his best friend, however, Mark decided to find out what Susan was asking of him. Mark didn't know it, but he and Susan had an age-old problem that could be helped by communicating more clearly. They needed to examine their individual sets of expectations about each other. Here's what they found out (after some time talking it out). In Susan's words:

Mark grew up in a doctor's home where his father had long and strange hours. The family ate their meals largely independent of the father's schedule; they usually could not keep up with all he had to do. So the idea of knowing when he would be around never crossed their minds. They planned their day without checking on his schedule, and he planned his without them. They made up for the family togetherness with weekend trips and projects. I, on the other hand, grew up in a small town on a farm. My dad worked long hours, but he always came in for meals at the same predictable time. The family planned to see each other at noon and at 5:00 p.m.; there was no question that my dad would be there. In fact, he was bothered if the meal was off schedule.

When I got married I thought all men worked like my father. I expected Mark to be in at mealtimes; and of course, reasonable mealtimes were noon and 5:00 p.m. When he left home without telling me what he was doing and when he would be back, I felt he was the most inconsiderate human being I had ever met. Mark, on the other hand, thought all men did just like him.

This type of misunderstanding happens when people forget that they are married to someone different from themselves. We grow up in families where we learn to do and to expect certain things. We forget that other families learn to do and to expect other things. Then when we "merge" into a new family as two adults, we forget to check out the signals and habits of our partner.

The need to learn about each other's expectations is another reason preparation for marriage is essential.

As a family, there is no single "right" way of doing things. There are no set rules that require particular jobs of one mate or the other. Old habits and past experiences tell us that some persons do one thing and others another. All these roles and expectations, however, have been learned.

The illusion that couples should know what to expect from each other is especially true with regard to sexuality. The best attitude and approach two persons can have toward each other is that of a student. An individual can only become a good partner to someone by learning about that person's ways and thoughts.

The need to learn about each other's expectations is another reason preparation for marriage is essential. It is impossible for a young man and a young woman to know much about each other in a short period of time. They must devote themselves to the chosen task of spending time learning from each other. They need to learn what the other person believes, has grown up with, prefers, dislikes, and cares about.

We cannot automatically know what other people expect and wish from life. We can, on the other hand, tell them what we expect and wish and share with them as we learn together how to hope, wish, and expect together as a couple (we'll talk about communicating our expectations in chapter 3).

False Idea 6: Men Think and Women Feel

Sally walked into my office and sat down with a jolt. I could tell she was frustrated. She volunteered to tell me that she was furious. What was she furious about?

"Do you know how hard it is to have to sound, look, and act dumber than boys?" she began. "That's what I have to do in order to get a date around here! These insecure little boys are so afraid of being challenged intellectually or emotionally that we girls have to pretend we're 'dumb blondes' in order not to damage their fragile egos. Do you know what happened to me this week? A guy I was just beginning to like very much stopped seeing me—after our first English papers came in. I happened to make the highest grade in the class. My best friend is dating him now, and she tells me that he just doesn't like 'smart girls.' Do I have to be stupid for a guy to feel comfortable with me?"

I started to assure Sally that there were a few young men around who would not be threatened by her intellectual abilities. She is one of many girls who struggle with this issue. Why? Because some people have been taught that men think—and women feel. The obvious truth is that both men and women feel and think!

The myth? Actually, there are two myths involved in the example of Sally. The first one is that men only think. Our culture has taught men for a long time to hide their feelings and express their thoughts. The result is a population of males who have trouble getting in touch with their feelings. They possess the same variety of feelings that women have. What they have learned to do is to mask them, swallow them, and camouflage them. As a result, an amazing number of men can only show certain feelings.

The "permissible" feelings that men regularly are allowed to express are anger and love (with reservations!). Some men don't even believe they have feelings of fear, pain, or sadness. They have been taught too well to ignore them. Somehow, as males develop, they begin to believe that they are "more rational" than women. This illusion is due largely to women's ability to experience and express feelings. The myth is accentuated because men have been programmed to be rational and intellectual.

The result? A generation or two of men who do not know how they feel. Many males have trouble recognizing and handling the feelings of women. The conditioning is so complete that some men actually believe they are born to be superior thinkers and that women have been born to be "feelers," with little sense and much nonsense.

The tragedy? Neither sex was designed to miss out on thinking or feeling. When men are trained to believe and act as if their feelings are unimportant, an entire portion of themselves is ignored. When women are treated as if they are mainly emotional luxuries, having no rational competence, an entire set of talents and abilities goes to waste.

The solution? Treat human beings as equals in the distribution of reason and emotion. Enhance man's ability to express his feelings. Increase women's opportunities to be seen as contributors to the intellectual and rational world.

―――――――――――――――――― **Stop and Think 10** ――――――――――――――――――

Look back at the marriage expectations you wrote earlier. Based on what you have just read, what expectations do you need to change or revise?

_____

_____

_____

True Words

How can we discover what we may expect and wish from each other as we think of marriage? One easy but important answer is that we discover by learning. Already, it has been suggested that a person who wants to take marriage seriously needs to be willing to become a student of his or her partner. What are some basic things to know as we explore the importance of expectations?

Truth 1: Each Person Has Different Needs

If we can accept and understand the fact that God has created no two people alike, then we will begin to accept the fact that no two people think alike. While some people want or expect certain things, others look for a different set of expectations.

Jake spends most of his day closely involved with people at the office. His job requires that he be a "troubleshooter," as many employees come to him for advice about handling personal problems and relationships. By the time Jake is on his way home, he is exhausted from relating to people.

Mary, Jake's wife, meanwhile, has been caring for three children who are under the age of seven. She looks forward to the moment when Jake arrives for her chance to talk to an adult. Yet, the first thing Jake does when he gets home is turn on the TV and sit down with the newspaper. He then tunes out everybody. Mary feels rejected and taken for granted.

What is happening in this household? Two partners meet each other at the end of the day with different sets of needs. If we could say it for them, here is what each one would say:

He: "I have had all the conversation I can handle for one day. Let me sit down, rest, and escape from all demands."

She: "I have been cooped up with children all day. Please talk to me as another adult."

Not only do individuals have different needs, but they also have different expectations about the same event. A husband wants to go to a movie to be alone with his wife; the wife is going because she's been wanting to get out of the house for two weeks.

Some persons have been reared to believe that a woman should never work outside the home, while others have known nothing but employed mothers. Some persons expect to share life with their mate alone. Others are far more interested in broadening their circle of friends as they marry. A few mates have grown up in families where disagreements were shouted out; others have grown up never expressing disagreements. One group will have an interesting time trying to understand the other.

These illustrations are meant to emphasize that what is expected and hoped as people view marriage has much to do with personal needs and attitudes. An individual who wants to share life with another person, therefore, must be prepared to learn what the mate expects of marriage. Those who take the time to find out are likely to be surprised by what they learn and will be doing a good job of avoiding surprises in their marriage!

Truth 2: Love Is Attitude and Will

A second important truth to learn about marriage is that relationships are held together by attitudes and will. A partner contributes to the development of the relationship by *encouraging* and *sustaining.* By encouraging positive responses, the partners reinforce the marriage.

The same is the case with the will. The moving force behind the start or the conclusion of a relationship is the will. Individuals choose to stay by someone and continue a relationship. They sustain an interest, and they establish growing commitments. When they decide to quit trying, they begin to discontinue the relationship. What they need to understand about people who marry is that they decide to commit and to remain together on the basis of a voluntary determination.

Hosea is a classic example of such love in the Old Testament. He had every reason to end the relationship with a wife who was unfaithful to him; yet he chose to stay by her. Though he did so at God's request, he willed to remain with her and to redeem the relationship. He was determined not to quit, and the love the couple rediscovered was largely possible because Hosea exercised this choice.

When we consider a Christian perspective on marriage, we are speaking of a commitment to shape attitudes and will to provide for the care and growth of a mate. So, as you consider whether or not marriage is for you, you need to train yourself to a new understanding of love. The presence of love (not moods of excitement) has much to do with our readiness to show attitudes of care and compassion. Love will be evident as we learn to work for the good of another person and as we learn to choose fidelity and vulnerability in a relationship.

Stop and Think 11

Read Matthew 19:4-6. What do these verses say about a Christian's responsibility to work to make a marriage succeed?

_____

_____

Truth 3: Two People Learn Together

What individuals promise to "do" in a marriage covenant is not simply to like what they know of each other. They are committing themselves to *grow and work through all the changes they will undergo together!* That is the substance of a Christian covenant: two people agreeing together to face the unknown future, based on their knowledge of each other and their conviction to remain together throughout the surprises of God's work in them.

As two individuals become a couple, they learn how to meet each new dimension of life together. Both individuals will be discovering new aspects of themselves; both will need to adjust to the new experiences and demands of each new stage in their lives. Both will learn together how to face each new challenge and to respond creatively to what is happening.

What we have been trying to say is that people should expect to change as they grow and learn. They also should expect their partner to change; for God has created all of us for constant development. These changes can be met if we understand the importance of keeping in touch with our mate. People who assume they know all they need to know about their partner lose out. They miss all the good new things God is revealing in the other's life. They grow apart from their partner.

Truth 4: Hopes and Dreams Should Be Explored

We dream differently at different times in life. The shared hopes we exchange in our teen years are rarely the hopes we share in our twenties. Nor are the wishes of the thirties and forties alike. Each stage of life provides a new set of visions. The sharing of those visions as they change and as they affect our lives is essential to a healthy husband-wife relationship.

Those who marry need to plan time and opportunities to share their dreams with each other. What does he believe a husband should be? How does she understand the image of a "husband"? What does she believe about a "wife"? What does he think a wife should be? These and other personal visions need to be exchanged, explored, discussed.

All our dreams shape what we expect from life and marriage. Young men and women seeking to take a relationship seriously must keep in constant touch with each other's visions. Sometimes people become depressed because they have quit dreaming—or because all their dreams are finished. Two partners talk:

"You haven't said much lately, Honey, and you seem depressed. What's happening? Are you discouraged about something?"

"Oh, I don't know. I guess I am depressed. I'm not sure what's going on. I just don't feel excited about anything. I guess I just don't have anything to care about. I'm bored. The kids are in school; the house is cleaned; there's no challenge at home; you're always busy. I want to do something worthwhile."

"What do you think you'd enjoy doing? After all, you're right: you've spent a great deal of time on our kids, being here when they needed you. Now they're busy, too. I'm sure you're ready for a new challenge."

These two people have just found each other right at a major crossroads in their shared life. They are about to explore a new horizon; they have wisely discovered that the wife's last horizon has been conquered. Each person needs regularly to explore boundaries, examine horizons. Marriage is a partnership in which two people assist each other in discovering their visions, completing them together, and seeking new ones under God's creative guidance. For the Lord of life is never a God of one vision; He is constantly calling us to our next dream with Him— and with the partner we are committed to—for life!

Stop and Think 12

Talk to an older married couple that you respect. Ask them how their dreams have changed through the years of their marriage and how they have shared their dreams with each other. Write what they said in summary form.

_____

_____

*H*OW DO I COMMUNICATE?

I promise to love, honor, cherish, share...

*D*iscovering who we are and exploring our expectations and dreams require communication. When we communicate, we are telling others who we are; and we are asking others who they are. How we communicate is vital. This chapter focuses on skills for sharing effectively with other persons and identifying purposes and goals as we communicate.[1]

Each of the areas dealt with in the following sections are helpful in understanding the art of sharing. Spend time asking yourself how well you understand the ideas presented. Each idea can help you develop effective ways of communicating.

Sharing What You Sense

All of us are equipped with five senses through which we perceive the world: sight, sound, smell, taste, and touch. These "receivers" help us know what is going on inside and out. They inform us about essential occurrences. We "read" the world through the assistance of these senses.

A visitor to western Texas was driving through a deserted portion of the state. His eyes caught a glimpse of a large, round object rolling across the highway directly in his path. Instinctively, he swerved the car to avoid the obstacle. He landed in the ditch beside the road. As he turned to see what he had avoided, he observed the "boulder" bump a rock and harmlessly roll on. It was a tumbleweed!

What happened to our friend in the car? He responded to one of his five senses (sight) and took action to avoid a problem. What he actually saw, however, and what he concluded in his mind were two different things. His brain was conditioned by years of caution to avoid large obstacles in his path. He concluded that it was a harmful object. His eyes, however, did not give him that information; his brain provided it, interpreting and adding to the visual perception.

What we need to train ourselves to do is to learn how to distinguish between "sense" perception and our interpretations of those senses. We see someone frowning; we say to ourselves, "*That person is frowning at me.*" Then we ask, "Why are you frowning at me?"

He replies: "The sun is in my eyes; I wasn't even looking at you."

A great amount of interpreting is done as we use our senses. Careful evaluation of what our senses tell us is a helpful way to start clear communication. The wife who was frustrated with her husband listened to him yell from the living room, "Honey, I'm proud of you." She replied, "I'm tired of you, too!" The ears did not fail to transmit the words; but the brain interfered and interpreted the message as the woman expected to hear it.

Stop and Think 13

Spend time this week noting the difference between what your senses pick up and interpretations you give the "messages." Record your impressions in the appropriate columns.

Statement	Your Immediate Interpretation	What was Meant
_____	_____	_____
_____	_____	_____
_____	_____	_____
_____	_____	_____

Evaluate your experiences by listing ways you mistranslated what you heard.

_____

_____

Sharing What You Think

If people were asked whether their thoughts affect how they perceive things, a number would say no. But we do allow our thoughts to "color" how we understand people, events, and information. When we look at a friend who is crying and say to ourselves or them, "What did I say wrong?" we are interpreting an event (with negative thoughts about our behavior). How do we know that the person is crying about something we did? What knowledge do we have about why that person is crying? What if we asked and were told: "Because I just received a letter from my mother, and she told me how much she loves me." New information increases our understanding.

We live and act based on what we think. Ask someone why he did something, and he replies, "I wasn't thinking." In reality the person could not have done anything without thinking about it. He just was not paying attention to his thoughts at the time. There is a big difference.

Indeed, our thoughts interpret our perceptions. We need to understand, then, that a great amount of what we believe needs to be checked for verification. A helpful tool of communication is the ability to listen to ourselves and to make distinctions between what others say and do and what we believe they said and did. Such careful investigation will save us from much misunderstanding.

George asked Katy out for Friday night. She said she was busy that evening with her family. On Friday George happened by Riverwood Mall and saw Katy in the pizza parlor with a group of people. Angered that she apparently lied to him, he stormed up to Katy and told her off. Later that night he found out that she was with her cousins from out of town. They were treating her to a pizza.

George did not check out his conclusions. He actually saw Katy in the pizza parlor. His mind added the additional mistaken interpretations. Many unnecessary problems are caused because we do not investigate our thoughts.

Sharing can add to clear communication. Asking people

what they are thinking is an easy way to avoid misunderstanding them. Good judgment involves asking ourselves if the thoughts we have about anything match the evidence we possess. Many times we have little evidence to support our assumptions. The only adequate remedy for our assumptions is checking instead of concluding. Our minds have been trained to make interpretations. What we need to learn to do is to pay attention to our thinking.

Our thoughts reflect how we see and understand the world. In order to tell others what we think, how we see things, and so on, we need to be able to share what is on our minds. Some people mistakenly search for a partner who can "read" their minds. They think, "If you really loved me you would know what I need." People who love may try harder, but no one can guess what someone else is thinking! The best gift we can offer someone we care for is to share our thoughts with that person. In such simple gestures lie the secrets of effective communication and mutual understanding.

Stop and Think 14

Describe a conflict that developed because you really did not communicate what you thought to your boyfriend (or girlfriend).

_____

_____

_____

What kind of communication would have kept the conflict from developing?

_____

_____

_____

Sharing What You Feel

With the exception of feelings based on physical events, all of our feelings are started by what we *think.* Understanding this truth helps us as we seek to share our feelings with others. A better understanding of how our feelings develop also is a helpful way to interpret and recognize them.

Charles had written Wanda six letters without a reply from her. When she left for camp she promised that she would write, that she would not allow the distance to isolate or alienate them. Charles wondered whether Wanda could keep loving him, especially surrounded by so many handsome male campers. The more he thought about it, the more he concluded that she was probably having a great time and was no longer interested in him.

If Wanda cared, Charles told himself several times, she would have at least written once. He then recalled nice things she had said to him about their relationship, and he began to treat them as deliberate lies. I've been played for a fool!

Angrily, Charles took pen and paper and wrote Wanda his "last letter." He told her how thoughtless and uncaring she was and how he hoped never to see her again. He said he was interested in other girls and suggested that their relationship be ended immediately. Two days after mailing the letter, Charles received a packet of six letters from the post office with a note that no one by that name was at the camp. In the same daily mail was a letter from Wanda from a different camp, asking him why he had not written her. Charles had mistakenly been using last year's camp address on all his letters.

Feelings are born in exactly that same manner every day. What we tell ourselves about people, situations, and experiences shapes our feelings within. To understand where those feelings come from can be a helpful way to understand ourselves and others.

We need to be consistent in communicating how we feel.

Some people sound angry when they are afraid; others shed tears when they are angry. A few people laugh when they are angry; and some people smile when they are angry. These are unclear ways of letting people know how we feel.

One useful exercise in communication is to ask others how they "read" our feelings. "Which feelings do you find easiest to understand in me?" is a favorite question young couples are asked to share. The next question is just as important, "What feelings are most difficult to detect in me?" Such shared thoughts do much to enhance communication between persons who care.

Those who share thoughts and feelings also need to assist each other in understanding the signals used to convey their feelings. Dating partners do well to offer to help each other learn how to "read" their feelings. Most people have learned to express their feelings in the family in which they grew up. Some families, for example, avoid open expressions of anger and withdraw when angry. Others learn to "blow up," while another group may cry when angry. The key to understanding a partner is the shared interpretation by both persons of how they deal with their feelings.

They promised to write to each other.

Stop and Think 15

Talk to someone of the opposite sex about how you share what you feel. Describe how they responded to your sharing.

_____

_____

_____

_____

_____

Learning to share feelings is a risky business, because it allows someone else to see us as we are. For that reason, the sharing of feelings is a gift of trust. Careful listening and exchanging of thoughts about feelings can become a tender experience in understanding another person.

Sharing What You Intend

A neglected aspect of communication relates to our intentions. We talk about our hopes and dreams only once in a while. We spend much time wishing for things yet never express our wishes. Good communication includes delivering our intentions to others.

Sharing hopes and intentions is an effective way to get them realized. When two persons care together about something, they can join efforts in seeing the dream realized. Consider Jennifer, for example. For seven years she had dreamed of going to Europe for a summer of study. Then she met Ralph, and the two decided to get married. Jennifer never mentioned her secret dream to Ralph. She quietly grieved the loss of a long-awaited hope. Every time they planned a vacation or spent money on any major project, Jennifer quietly resented the plan. Finally, Ralph asked her why she was so negative about holiday plans. In a burst of honest emotion, Jennifer revealed her private intentions of traveling to Europe. By the following summer she was able to make her trip.

Persons who consider marriage need to learn to share their aspirations and dreams about who they want to become. They can express dreams about their future and exchange potential goals they hope to accomplish. They should discuss important issues, such as whether or not they want to be parents and how many children are in their plans for the future. All these private dreams are windows into the soul. The willingness to share is a mark of trust in the relationship and an important contribution toward clearer understandings of each other.

Personal wishes should also be the subject of shared conversation. So many young couples wish for certain appropriate things from each other but do not spell them out. One young man is hungry for personal affirmation and affection. He wishes that his wife would come up to him, hug him, and say something tender to him. Yet to tell her what he wants, he believes, would ruin the experience. A young lady, in her loneliness, wishes that someone would call her or tell her that he cares. She waits. If she herself called someone, a new relationship probably would develop for two people.

Many times our intentions are not pursued by actions or words that would make them possible. A world of needs, aspirations, and ambitions lives within us; to share them with someone is to communicate about important matters. People who develop balanced relationships share their hopes and dreams!

Stop and Think 16

List several of your hopes and dreams for the future.

_____

_____

Share these hopes and dreams with a friend of the opposite sex.

Shared life is expressed in thoughts, feelings, intentions, and actions.

Sharing Through Actions

In order to be understood well, we need to share how we feel through our actions. The young man who looks feverishly for a job in order to buy an engagement ring is saying something significant about his plans. A young lady who takes courses year-round in order to finish college in less than three years is communicating about her purposes. Shared life is expressed in thoughts, feelings, intentions—and actions.

The young man who continually reassures his girlfriend that she is his only interest yet shows up frequently in public places with other dates contradicts himself with his behavior. The young woman who puts off conversations about marriage and engagement every time they are brought up is saying something about her fear of a permanent commitment.

Good communication involves actions that reflect what we say and think. Sometimes our deeds are consistent with our thoughts, words, and wishes. At other times, we contradict what we say by what we do. Consider the young man who talks about how he wants to know his date better but regularly takes her to activities in which little conversation is required (movies, football games, dances, and so forth).

Phil and Jodi had been seeing each other for six months. Phil told her he loved her and planned to marry her. Jodi was uneasy about Phil, though. Most of their dates were spent in physical "petting" and little conversation. One day Jodi interrupted their affections to tell Phil that she wanted to spend more time talking and getting to know how he felt about some things. Phil became angry, drove Jodi home immediately, and never saw her again.

Often people express their love with gifts. The bouquet of flowers, box of candy, and surprise present are familiar tokens of affection. Those who care also show their feelings by hugging, placing an arm around the shoulder or waist, and holding hands. The most important thing to learn about actions and gestures is that what we do should be consistent with how we feel.

Many couples become involved in premarital sexual activity supposedly because they are "in love." A more careful examination of their feelings often reveals one of two things: (1) They desire physical affection and use sexual behavior as a way of getting physical affirmation. (2) They do not understand the nature of sexual intimacy as a unique communion between two people in a mutual commitment. Thus they engage in sexual activity as an emotional "high," using the behavior as recreation or entertainment.

Our actions and deeds have much to do with communication. When we desire to share our life with someone else, we will want to reflect on and interpret our actions. We also will want to understand the behavior or actions of the other person. Good communication involves the sharing of thoughts, perceptions, feelings, intentions, and actions. Love is the mutual commitment to know each other and to care and nurture what is known. The better we communicate, therefore, the more thoroughly we can love!

Stop and Think 17

Name ways you communicate your thoughts and feelings through your actions.

_____

_____

_____

Are your actions understood correctly? If not, what can you do to make sure your actions communicate your true thoughts and feelings?

_____

_____

_____

What helpful tips for effective communication did you learn from studying this chapter? List several.

_____

_____

_____

How can these tips help you prepare for marriage?

_____

_____

[1]The concepts developed in this chapter grow out of the author's experiences with the content of a book by Miller, Nunnally, and Wackman entitled *Alive and Aware*.

WHAT DO I BELIEVE AND LIVE BY?

*A*dequate preparation for life requires an understanding of priorities, the beliefs we consider most important. These beliefs determine how we live and spend our time. The careful choosing of these beliefs is a major process of development that occurs in the late teen years and the early twenties. In that process, some of the beliefs and values we have heard about all our lives become ours in a very personal way.

Selecting personal values is essential preparation for sharing life with another person. What will we believe and live by? STOP AND THINK about your beliefs. In the exercise that follows list the beliefs that are most important to you—the beliefs you would not give up under any circumstances.

Stop and Think 18

What beliefs and values are most important to you? List several.

_____

_____

_____

_____

What Is Most Important in Life?

Priorities—what we consider most important—determine the person we will be; they also help us select the quality of person with whom we wish to link our life. That is why a careful, personal assessment of our priorities is important.

Our priorities must also be our values. The beliefs and values held by our parents may be adequate for them. We, however, must live by our own chosen beliefs. Unless we choose beliefs for ourselves, they will be like secondhand clothes and will not survive to guide us. The committed Christian has a set of beliefs that guide life in a particular way. What are the beliefs and values that shape the life of a Christian?

Creator and Creature

A basic Christian belief is that we do not answer to ourselves alone for how we live. We report back to the Author of life, who has designed us with specific purposes. A central truth for Christians is that we do not live for our own purposes but respond to a higher purpose. In so doing, we seek to follow the will and plan of our Creator.

Belief in a Creator also means we believe that God shares life with us. As Christians, therefore, we always acknowledge three team members in a marriage relationship: God, husband, and wife. Any potential partner for a Christian must be aware of this fact. That is why so many church people suggest that believers seek believers as mates. The difference between Christians and non-Christians in regard to this basic issue is significant. Believers see marriage as a double responsibility: we answer to God and to our partner. We affirm the principles whereby God governs life.

Commitment and Cooperation

Those who promote a Christian point of view assume that marriage is a once-in-a-lifetime commitment. We choose a mate carefully because we intend to live with that person for life. Marriage is a venture to be fully shared; for the Scriptures indicate that man and woman are to be help mates for each other. Those who commit themselves to marriage understand that what they are doing is a lifetime commitment.

=================== Stop and Think 19 ===================

Read Genesis 2:24. What does this verse say about marriage as a lifetime commitment?

_____

_____

_____

_____

Christians affirm their participation in a wider community.

Community and Fellowship

Our biblical value system does not endorse the idea of living for oneself or even for one's mate alone. Christians affirm their participation in a wider community, a family of God to whom we are related. As you consider your part in the biblical value system, you should understand that we should share all we are with this wider family. We are nurtured by this community and by the God who is the Father of this fellowship. We worship together for nourishment and support. We offer our gifts and abilities through this community, and we gain nurture and love from its fellowship.

Stewardship and Possessions

As believers in a God who owns all, we share our financial and personal resources for God's work. We do so as an affirmation that what we have belongs to God and that we are merely "stewards" or managers of our possessions. Anyone who considers sharing life with a Christian should know how dramatically such a belief affects the economic plans of a Christian. Material possessions, for those who assume this value, are always instruments of service for the good of people. They are not to replace people in importance.

Calling and Vocation

A belief system with long-term meaning has something to say about the jobs we choose. According to a Christian perspective on vocations, every work an individual does should be consistent with God's purposes and goals. Accordingly, you and your future partner will need to consider your understanding of vocational plans and what God would have you be and do. Christians believe in a special "call" from God. Those who assume this belief value will always evaluate future work positions in light of the Christian context: Is this a job God has prepared me for? Is it in keeping with His goals for my life? (This subject will be discussed in more detail in chapter 7.)

Integrity

A serious evaluation of beliefs must come to terms with the issue of integrity. Many options ignore a responsible commitment to honesty and personal faithfulness to truth. We who are committed to the Christian viewpoint must face such a requirement. The biblical perspective on relationships makes total honesty and personal reliability essential. We give our word as a binding covenant that we have spoken the truth. The God who stands for truth and integrity is our model. All human relationships, especially the marital partnership, assume this value.

Jesus Christ

Any affirmation that accepts the existence of the Creator must also deal with the fact of Jesus Christ. Our value orientation declares that He is the full revelation of God in human form. We believe that He is the model for living and that His presence in our world communicates His love for us. We believe He offered His life to the point of death; and, to follow Him as THE WAY of life, we must be prepared to offer our lives. Such a commitment is central to all our values. These realities need to be understood by anyone who plans to share life with a Christian partner.

The meaning of Jesus Christ is an issue that should be discussed. What you decide about Jesus Christ has enormous implications for your life. Christians affirm that Jesus Christ represents God as fully as can be expressed in human ways. We also believe that Jesus is the one who gives us the way of contact and renewed relationship with God.

Stop and Think 20

What do you believe about Jesus Christ?

_____

_____

What does the person you are dating believe about Jesus Christ?

_____

_____

(If you don't know, ask the person and write her or his response here.)

_____

_____

Holy Spirit

The presence of God within us and among us and others is another significant affirmation. We who choose a value system must decide if the presence of God is that of a being far away, or if He is one who inhabits us and our relationships from within. Since He is one who lives in our midst, then who we are, what we do, and what happens between us and other people is affected by His presence. As Christians, we believe we can call upon the power of the Holy Spirit to bring about an atmosphere of peace, love, joy, patience, tenderness, goodness, fidelity, and self-control. Such a value system assumes that we are not alone in the trials and triumphs of life.

Pilgrimage

Different points of view suggest how we should live life on earth. Some people propose that life is mainly a treadmill with no purpose. Others claim that life is repetitive, with no progress. Still others think of living as a constant, uphill battle. Christians understand life as a pilgrimage.

Pilgrimages begin with commitments and encounters, such as Abraham had with God (see Gen. 12:1-7). They reflect more than a point in time, however; they speak of a walk that is continuous. This walk is called "the Way" in the New Testament (Acts 16:17; 18:26) and involves progress, destination, and companionship. As Christians, we believe that we have a lifetime to get where we are going. We also believe that a commitment begins with "I do" or "I will." We see life, from that moment on, as a walk with God toward the full establishment of His kingdom. That walk involves learning, developing, nurturing, achieving, failing, forgiving, and hoping.

Pilgrimages are not made alone. The people of God walk together in companionship. We are promised Christ's presence throughout the journey. We are not protected from life, but we find strength to make the journey through God's presence, strength, encouragement, and commitment. An important value to be considered is the issue of seeing life as a pilgrimage toward perfect purpose!

The Bible

For the Christian the single source in matters of faith and practice is the Bible. In this book we find God's revelation in history, encounter the person of Jesus Christ, and receive God's gifts of grace and resurrection. When an individual selects a person with whom he or she might share life, it is important to know how that person feels about the Scriptures.

Knowing what favorite passages inspire a partner may also be revealing about the person's faith. Sharing our understanding of the Scriptures likewise can be an inspiration to the relationship.

Church

Church provides community for a believer. Christians live as a people in families by God's design. The church was destined to be a fellowship of people who are knit together by one common Father. We call each other brother and sister because of that bond.

As you and persons close to you begin to share what is important, ask each other what church means to you. Ask others in your circle of friendship. The church was designed to be a family of love, bonded together, learning together, sustaining together, proclaiming God's grace together, and growing together.

Forgiveness and Grace

Any relationship grounded on Christian principles includes forgiveness. The same God, who daily forgives us, calls us to forgive one another. All human experiences, for believers, are grounded on the ability to continuously pardon other people. This issue is crucial in potential marital relationships; for it implies that both mates stand on the same ground. All humans are sinners. The issue of forgiveness, then, is one of offering the same grace that Jesus Christ offers us. One day one partner will need to be forgiven; the next day the other may need grace.

This mutuality of forgiveness also means that there are no relationships based on superiority or ranking of importance. The God who claims all children as having the same worth demands that those who take on His values see one another as equals in all respects (Gal. 3:28). Grace also means that we are to forgive without limit—"seventy times seven" (Matt. 18:22). For the Christian partner, grace means that he or she will forgive and start over many times.

All these principles shape the outlook and priorities of a

believing mate. As you determine what you will live by, take all these matters into consideration and then consider how important the beliefs of a future partner may be in affecting your Christian life-style.

Stop and Think 21

Listed below are the categories just discussed. Write one sentence that expresses your belief related to each category.

Creator and Creature _____

Commitment and Cooperation _____

Community and Fellowship _____

Stewardship and Possessions _____

Calling and Vocation _____

Integrity _____

Jesus Christ _____

Holy Spirit _____

The Bible _____

Church _____

Forgiveness and Grace _____

How can the communication guidelines you learned in chapter 3 help you in sharing these beliefs with a potential mate?

_____

What Does My Faith Say About Marriage?

The word *faith* has several meanings. In this book, faith is that belief within an individual that affects all of life. As Christians, we stake our lives and futures on the fact that a God who loves us has come to us in Jesus Christ. We believe Jesus' coming was an event that saves us from a life without purpose. We also believe that Christ's saving power remains with us to sustain us in all circumstances of life. Do your particular values "hang" on reliable truths?

Faith is like a verb because it is a continuous experience. It is an active encounter that the believer experiences daily in a walk already described as a "pilgrimage." Faith is developed on this walk and is strengthened by this walk. Faith is a growing trust and affirmation that what a person has staked life on is actually taking place. At the same time, faith is belief before event.

Faith makes possible a confident walk into an unknown future. Through faith the mystery of our future can be trusted. We believe with conviction that God is in our future with us. Facing the unknown with Christ becomes more of an adventure and less a dread.

The importance of such an outlook is crucial to marriage. Marriage itself is an act of faith; for no one can know in advance what will take place in the future of a relationship. In marriage, faith comes to sustain us constantly. Having done all we can to know the person we selected under God for marriage, we then trust God for our future. He will be more than adequate for any surprises that life brings.

She married him understanding that their God was calling him to special service. When he wrote to ask for her hand and companionship in another country, she responded with: "Entreat me not to leave you or return from following you; for where you go I will go, and where you lodge I will lodge; your people shall be my people, and your God my God; where you die I will die, and there will I be buried. May the Lord do so to me and more also if even death parts me from you" (Ruth 1:16-17, RSV).

Then many years later, he looked into her teary eyes. They had moved to a country six thousand miles away from family, and had been there for stretches of twelve years. Two children had died at birth; a promising young son drowned saving his friends. She had just received news that her oldest boy disappeared from medical school in Galveston. They had known many surprises in their fifty years of marriage. And, as his eyes met hers again, wondering how she felt, he heard her whisper: "Entreat me not." (Ann and William Buck Bagby, grandparents of the writer).

Faith is the essential ingredient that enables young men and women to affirm with confidence that they will face life together. They know that they can overcome all stress and unexpected misfortune. The Lord of life will walk with them: "Lo, I am with you always, even to the end of the age" (Matt. 28:20).

Faith makes possible a confident walk into an unknown future.

================== **Stop and Think 22** ==================

Express in your own words the part faith plays in the decision to marry and in decisions made as a couple after marrying.

_____

_____

_____

What Do I Want a Partner to Believe?

In answering this question, perhaps the first thing that needs to be stated is that *marriage does not require finding a person who has one's identical set of beliefs.* God has never expected everyone to see things exactly alike. However, there are basics to our faith that make for harmony.

What people value and live by is crucial. Yet, so many marriages take place without a whisper of exchanged ideas about beliefs. Why do we spend so little time discussing this topic? Some think we avoid the subject because we believe that values are a private matter, not too easily discussed. By the time one individual is getting serious about another, though, he or she certainly should be getting inquisitive about this matter. To understand what a potential marriage partner believes, take the time to ask.

Baptists believe in the "priesthood of the believer." That means each person is his or her own representative before God. This belief also implies that each of us answers to our own understanding of the truth. We are responsible for how revelation has come to us personally.

When we seek to understand another person's values, then, we need to give that person room to see things somewhat differently from the way we do. We need to appreciate how God has spoken to that individual. We also need to understand that different people are traveling at different places in the journey with God. To require that someone see things as we do is to

Take the time to ask what a potential marriage partner believes.

deny that person his or her own place in God's pilgrimage.

One helpful experience for those who are dating persons of other faiths is to discuss what each one believes. A visit to worship events with a person we care about can be revealing and instructive, creating good conversation and questions for both to explore. People with differing religious backgrounds need to understand that they can differ without offending each other. To be pleasant and respectful is important in questions of faith and values.

As we consider the future and a life shared with another person, it will be helpful to arrive at some basic issues that are "nonnegotiable." That means: *What have I decided about my belief system that I cannot give up—or change?* Such a discovery will assist us in deciding what we need to pay attention to as we talk seriously with a partner about what he or she believes.

Marriage to a person with contrasting values is a problem. Persons who have tried to dismiss such differences have found them hard to overcome. Many fine young people discover that beliefs they were supposedly willing to give up because they were in love are not so easily set aside. The most frequent time when such differences reemerge is at the point when children are old enough to "go to church." Where will they go? The beliefs and values of many years return to speak strongly at such times and need to be explored before they become the cause of much pain and sorrow.

The importance of clear communication once again appears. Couples who are beginning to care deeply for each other need to examine their priorities and values. The accepting, open atmosphere of a dialogue in which both people can share what they live by is ideal. The importance of discussing the issues that guide our lives cannot be overemphasized.

Some young people find it helpful to sit down and discuss their beliefs with their ministers. Such discussion is especially helpful when two persons of different faiths are involved. Remember that a pastor's commitment to God makes him a valuable resource as individuals examine and evaluate their beliefs.

Stop and Think 23

Look back at your responses to the question in Stop and Think 18. Revise your answers based on what you have read in this chapter. Then list below the beliefs you hold that are "nonnegotiable" (cannot give up or change).

_____

_____

What do you want the person you marry to believe?

_____

_____

If you are seriously dating someone, share with that person what you wrote here.

Chapter 5

WHAT KIND OF MANAGER AM I?

*B*aseball managers, hotel managers, store managers, general managers—you've heard these titles. Persons with titles like these make sure things are handled properly. They are placed in charge to coordinate people or property for effective use.

Managers are not necessarily owners. But, even though they may not own the things they handle, they are responsible for them. They report to the owner about how merchandise, projects, or people carry out the owner's intentions. They also make sure everything they manage works well together. In that sense, they are like an orchestra conductor, whose main function is to help a group of musicians play the music together.

Establishing a Management Viewpoint

Christians believe God owns all that He has created. The world and everything in it belongs to Him. In the beginning, God directed people to "manage" His created order (see Gen. 1:26-31). God made it clear that man and woman were to be responsible for all that He placed in their hands. Believers, therefore, think of their money and "possessions" as actually belonging to God. We consider ourselves caretakers (stewards) of His property and, as such, responsible for how we use it. That is why, in church circles, Christians talk about being "stewards" of God's money. We believe He wants us to use it wisely.

Students of the Bible use the word *tithe* to speak about a practice that is important to God's people. The Bible teaches that God wants us to share from our earnings so that at least 10 percent goes to His work through the church (Mal. 3:8-10). God instructed the Israelites to leave some of their harvest for the poor and the priests (Deut. 14:22-29). He wanted His property shared with the needy and with those who worked for His worship and ministry. One main function of sharing resources in a common "collection" is that Christians can cooperate to contribute to a cause we could not financially support by ourselves. When missionaries are sent out by a "cooperative" effort, many believers share in that ministry.

Because we are committed to the principle that all the money we manage actually belongs to God, we become more and more concerned with giving part of it back for God's cooperative mission. Some faithful stewards, using the 10 percent example as a minimum standard, go beyond that and give more for God's work.

Any person who is considering marriage needs to understand how a person thinks about money. The believer who is getting serious in a relationship needs to know what kind of commitments influence how the other person manages money. Someone who believes that he can use his salary as he pleases will have conflict with a believer who understands herself as a manager for God.

Likewise, a potential partner who thinks of her or his salary as accountable to the partner only, may be surprised to discover that the Christian partner wants to ask about God's will in regard to the salary. One frequent argument among young married couples concerns whether any money is going to be given to the church and how much.

"John, I told you yesterday that we wouldn't have the money for a new lawn mower until next month. We haven't given a cent to the church this month, and you know how important that is to me!"

"Well, Sarah, it may be important to you, but the lawn just wasn't going to wait until next month. So I had to buy a mower. The Lord understands these things. He won't mind waiting a month or two. Anyway, we've given enough to the church to keep it going for a long time!"

"Now just what does that mean? Are you implying that we are breaking our necks to give God what is His already? I thought we went over that just a few months ago. If we are so tight, why do we have a new car in the garage?"

"Wait just a minute, Sarah! The car in the garage doesn't have anything to do with God. I'm talking about how our lawn mower is about to die and how much we give to the church anyway."

The issue in that conversation was not whether there was enough money to go around but how those two people felt about the way to spend their money. One person had strong feelings about giving to the church. The partner strongly opposed that view. In this case, the religious belief of one person was not shared by the other. Those who consider becoming marriage partners need to take into account the fact that religious beliefs affect how people use their money. Most individuals don't change beliefs that are important to them. What a person believes about money and how it should be managed is important.

Stop and Think 24

How do you feel about giving money to your church?

_____

Have you shared your feelings with your steady date? If so, what was that person's response?

_____

_____

Facing Financial Reality

To manage money properly, potential marriage partners must have enough money to manage! Some young couples contemplate marriage with a positive attitude and no employment. When asked how they plan to support themselves, they say, "We'll manage!" As clever as that sounds, they really don't have anything to manage.

Marriages can survive without "established" incomes. However, a sound way to plan for marriage is to have a stable income. Enough anxiety and uncertainty is present in the experience of marriage without having to worry about money to live on. Couples who get married and then seek employment say time after time how much they wished they had waited just long enough to feel secure. Unemployment and constant job changes are sources of insecurity and irritation in a young marriage.

Couples sometimes plan to marry with the understanding

that parents will provide for them financially at first. While that plan can be a workable, temporary solution, it fails about twice as much as it works. Why? Because young partners who are dependent on parents financially find it much more difficult to "set up house" apart from the parents. Financial dependence almost always breeds emotional or personal dependence. Sometimes the couple feels obligated in certain ways, whether or not the lending parents make them feel obligated. At other times the parents who lend, subtly or openly, place uncomfortable pressure on the bride or groom. For these reasons, it is strongly recommended that those who plan for marriage spend time determining ways to support themselves from the beginning.

Two special issues deserve a comment. Frequently, marrying partners are completing their education. Sometimes parents who have promised to pay for their son or daughter's education volunteer to complete that plan after marriage. Such a generous offer is appropriate. A clear understanding of the extent of the assistance and its conclusion should be agreed upon by the parents and the couple.

Some parents are sensitive enough to "back away" as young people marry. They thus allow the couple to gain confidence in their own ability to support themselves financially. Yet the older couple, established financially, may wish from time to time to offer a special gift to assist the young couple. Proud and independent young men and women may resist these offers as if their souls are being bought. Perhaps they should investigate the motives behind such gestures before they reject them. Most parents have only the purest love and a desire to help. Caring parents should be able to offer special gifts without endangering either the young couples' self-esteem or freedom. Sensitivity and understanding with such gestures will deepen the relationship between parents and the couple.

Surveying Assets and Liabilities

What is a beginning point for money management in a marriage? First and foremost, a couple should be open about how

Couples should let each other know about assets and liabilities.

much money they have and how much money they owe. Couples considering marriage need to let each other know about their assets and liabilities. Assets are all the possessions and money that a person owns. Liabilities are all the debts and bills an individual has. Marriage partners are entitled to know what debts they are taking on when they marry and what money is available for the partnership.

Marriage does not require that all money owned become a "common pot." The need for honesty about all money owned, however, is essential. One person may tell the other that property she has inherited needs to remain in her name. She may explain that she has made a commitment to her family to use it in a certain way. Another partner may have a savings account that the family has contributed to for years. If the savings was for a particular purpose, then the couple can share in discussing the dream. Money commitments made prior to marriage plans can and should be honored. What is necessary is that no secret or private plans be made by either partner. Hidden plans create suspicion and misunderstanding.

Developing a Spending Plan

When two individuals discuss the possibility of marriage, they are talking about going into a financial partnership, a merging of two different ways of thinking about money matters. Each family handles money in a unique way. The families of the two mates have taught them much about how to manage money. Now they are about to discover a way of "pooling" knowledge with a new financial partner.

Discussions about ways potential mates use money can be helpful in understanding how each one thinks about money. Such conversations are a natural part of planning and preparing for marriage. Do both individuals believe in a dual income, or does one mate think only one should work outside the home? If only one mate "makes the money," how do both of them see that money? Is it "his," "hers," or "ours"? If both work outside the home, do both incomes go into a common fund? Do the partners want to spend their money independently? If so, will they also divide costs equally?

Another important factor in money management is the household budget. A budget is an itemized plan for how a person or family will spend their money. Couples often are surprised that there are so many different ways to distribute money.

One helpful money-management exercise is for two potential marriage partners to make separate lists of how they would spend their income. Comparing budgets allows the couple to see how alike and differently they would distribute the family budget. Usually, most of the first items are similar. A few "unique" items appear farther down the list. The lists of items gives each person a chance to see how much the partner would spend on a particular item. Each person then has a better idea of how the partner feels about the importance of certain items.

═══════════════ **Stop and Think 25** ═══════════════

Develop a make-believe budget using the following list of items and available income of $2000 per month. Ask the person you are dating to do the same. Then compare budgets.

apartment	car
entertainment	church
clothes	gas
doctors	furniture
food	insurance
savings	laundry

Now compare the list you just made with the following "budgets" that were developed by a couple recently involved in premarital counseling. Two-source available income was $2000.

His		**Hers**	
apartment	$500.00	house	$800.00
car	500.00	food	300.00
food	200.00	clothes	100.00
entertainment	150.00	car	500.00
insurance	50.00	school	100.00
clothes	50.00	transportation	80.00
gas	150.00	savings	50.00
recreation	50.00	church	100.00
savings	50.00	laundry	20.00
doctors	40.00	doctors	30.00
furniture	100.00	household	80.00
	$1840.00		$2160.00

The first thing this couple noticed was that he had money left over, and she had overspent. Careful checking revealed why. The husband expected to spend quite a bit less on housing than the wife. After noticing this difference, they discussed their views about what kind of house they would live in at first.

A second item that had significantly different totals was food. The wife felt that more money would be needed for food. A good exercise in this area is to have two marriage partners take a grocery-shopping trip together. Experience will reveal that the wife was more in line with what couples spend for food.

Further helpful conversation came at several other points in the budget study. The husband planned generously for recreation and entertainment, telling his wife that these items were important in his daily life. She planned for a church offering and indicated that it was important to her.

Additional study of this budget will show that both individuals left off some items. Couples not only can help each other by suggesting budget needs overlooked, but they also can discuss which items are most important. Those who spend time discussing these matters usually understand each other better. How we spend our money says a lot about who we are and what we value.

The chance to discuss a budget raises the important question of debts. Will these two people spend only what they make, or will they go into debt to secure what they want? A frequent problem young married couples face today is owing more than they can pay. Many are not willing to wait for what they want as long as couples did a number of years ago. In order to get what they want immediately, couples buy on monthly installments. Such payments are an excellent way to purchase major items that they would not be able to afford immediately. The main problem with installment buying, though, is that it becomes a "fixed" bill each month just like a water bill. While one or two monthly bills are affordable, several bills may cause a heavy financial burden. Couples who charge items and start several monthly payments soon are spending more per month than they are bringing in.

Keeping Financial Records

Many marriage partners use a checking account to keep track of their money. Banks mail monthly statements that tell customers the status of their accounts—money deposited and spent, banking charges, and the balance of the account. Joint checking accounts offer the symbolic advantage of making a couple feel like the money they handle is theirs together.

The question of who pays the bills and keeps the financial records and the checkbook is important, because some people are good with records and others are not. In addition, some feel the need to control the money management in their family. The stereotype that men know more about finances than women is happily passing from the scene. Evidence points to the fact that it simply depends on each person. Some men and some

Decisions must be made about who keeps the financial records.

women are excellent record keepers. Some men and some women are poor record keepers. Good management requires responsible record keeping. People who have been able to "get by" before marriage need to realize that adequate family living depends on keeping careful financial records. Whatever way couples choose to use a checking account, both partners should be aware of the money distribution.

In addition to being a vehicle for keeping financial records, a checking account also protects the owners from theft. Further, young people need to consider the safety of their belongings and valuable items. A bank safe-deposit box is a good place to store valuable items that are not needed regularly.

Stop and Think 26

How do you feel about making purchases on the monthly-installment plan?

_____

Who should keep track of the checkbook? Why?

_____

_____

Share your answers with a friend for comparison of ideas.

Sharing Feelings About Money

Couples should discuss how they both feel about the use of money. Some individuals feel free to use money as the occasion demands, while others are cautious about spending. It is important that marriage partners have a certain amount of spending money that they are not expected to report to anyone. Every human being is entitled to a little privacy, and couples do well to discuss the importance of having some funds that each partner alone can spend. A sense of self-worth, personal identity, and private choosing is encouraged when marriage partners allow each other some freedom with funds. Naturally, the amount of such "mad" money will vary, depending on the budget.

Jackie and Tom had been married for two years. They enjoyed most aspects of marriage; but, from time to time, Jackie complained that there never was enough money to buy what she needed. Tom could not understand her problem because she, after all, kept the checkbook with her. He felt that they were living within their income and could not understand why she felt confined.

One day, as they were visiting with Jackie's parents, Tom discovered that she grew up in a family where all members had a separate checking account. He, on the other hand, grew up with a common checking account for the entire family. When anyone in Tom's family needed money, the person took as he or she required. In Jackie's family, members used only what they held individually in their accounts.

When Tom and Jackie returned home, they discussed the fact that Jackie could never feel comfortable taking money from a joint account because it was not hers. The couple then agreed on a solution. Each time the paycheck came in, Jackie would take an agreed upon sum ($60) that was hers to spend as she needed. The rest remained in the checking account, where Tom still felt the freedom to spend. For the first time in their marriage, Jackie did not feel financially trapped.

While "private" money is appropriate, good money managers consult with partners before making major purchases. A "major" expense would involve more than $50.00. Emergencies, of course, are another matter.

Those who learn to be sensitive to the emotional value behind the use of money will better understand and appreciate their partner. The man who has always helped pay his aging father's car expenses should be heard for the tender motives behind his actions. He is not just being irresponsible with the new

Good money managers consult with partners before making major purchases.

couple's limited finances. Rather, he may feel that he has a lifelong commitment to his father. The two need to discuss this expenditure in order to understand feelings.

A healthy conversation between partners can avoid much "underground" anger. The young woman who has never borrowed from her parents may have genuine reservations about making such a request of them after she is married. Partners who talk about what they are comfortable with and how they feel about the way money is spent can work through their differences.

Ignoring how one mate feels about money can cause problems in the relationship. When a partner in a marriage feels ignored or slighted, it is common to see that person "take it out" on the checkbook. Studies on marriage stress indicate that one of the favorite ways for mates to show their anger indirectly is to spend money.

Planning for the Future

Discussions about planning in the present lead to concerns about planning for the future. What issues should be raised as young men and women look to the future financially?

People who consider the future will plan better financially if they include a savings plan that takes into account their long-range needs. Most couples today enter marriage with good insights about housing. They know that people who buy homes fare better financially than people who rent. While most couples need to rent an apartment or home at first, their vision for the first 10 years of marriage should include the down payment and purchase of a home. This planning requires sacrifice. Yet, thoughtful planning will make it possible for a couple to own property and save money during the early years of marriage. Each young family needs to plan for a home in accordance with income, moving possibilities, and available opportunities.

A smart plan for the future evaluates the transportation needs of the family "down the road." New partners not only need to discuss whether they will be a one- or two-car family tomorrow, they also need to evaluate long-term family needs. If available transportation allows a couple to avoid the purchase of a car, they are wise to do so. Several practical matters need to be raised when assessing the purchase of a car: employment, public transportation, carpooling, distance from home, arrival of children, and so forth. Wise marital partners set money aside for the purchase of the transportation they have deemed necessary.

The advent of children is another important financial consideration for the long-range forecast. Estimates in the nineties indicate that each child born will require about $95,000 to deliver debt free out of college! Such a staggering bill need not overwhelm potential marriage candidates. The bill on this "complete child rearing" is spread over approximately 25 years. Still, each child considered being brought into a young couples' home should be understood for its financial cost. The dividends and assets of having children, of course, far outweigh this figure! For this reason many couples begin planning years in advance for their children's education or for braces or other needs.

Retirement may seem like an ugly, distant word to young people. But smart financial planning provides for a retirement income and life insurance. Reliable financial planners are available for counsel on these matters. Finding insurance coverage for a young family in case the husband or wife is incapacitated is important. People who plan for the future consider these needs and decide together on the course of action that best fits their circumstances.

Sound financial planning also will include a serious look at medical insurance. As the family enlarges, the need for adequate coverage makes health assistance a vital issue in planning for the future. Many established jobs provide these benefits automatically. Potential partners need to discuss their feelings about such matters.

One additional issue needs to be mentioned. Although the need to care for aging parents may seem remote at this point, the subject deserves thoughtful anticipation. How do potential mates feel about the care of their parents in later years? Academic as the question may seem, it often surfaces much earlier than expected. To know and to understand how a husband or wife feels about the finances of such decisions can be revealing and significant. Here is a true account of one person's response.

Somehow I never thought it would be like this. Sure, I knew Bert's parents didn't have much money and were quite a bit older than mine. But I always thought that, when the time came and they could not take care of themselves, his brothers would be eager to take them in. That didn't happen. I guess I also thought we would place them in a home where they could be properly cared for. I never thought they would live with us. Our privacy is gone now— maybe for as long as we're strong. Our savings have been depleted from adding one room to the house so they could live here. And now, she's about to go into the hospital, and they have no insurance! What are we going to do?

Certainly, no young candidate for marriage wants to examine all future needs in one sitting. Nor can a couple plan for all events. What has been suggested here is that some planning is responsible, helpful, and peace producing. We still face tomorrow by faith. When we have done our best to plan and to conduct our business as good stewards, then Christ's admonition in the Sermon on the Mount can reassure us from the proper context: "Do not be anxious then, saying, 'What shall we eat?' or 'What shall we drink?' or 'With what shall we clothe ourselves?' For all these things the Gentiles eagerly seek; for your heavenly Father knows that you need all these things. But seek first His kingdom and His righteousness; and all these things shall be added to you" (Matt. 6:31-33, NASB).

Stop and Think 27

Write at least one action a couple needs to take to plan for the future in the following areas.

Savings _____

Transportation _____

Children _____

Retirement _____

Insurance _____

Care for aging parents _____

HOW DO I EXPRESS MY SEXUALITY?

*S*exuality is neither an act nor an "appetite," as labeled by some who study behavior. We are sexual creatures, male and female. Our sexuality is our identity. As sexual creatures we have been formed with two basic identities. Sexual man and sexual woman are designed differently physically and functionally. At the same time, we share common feelings and common capacities for learning.

Stop and Think 28

Write your definition of sexuality.

_____

Revise your definition after you have read this chapter.

_____

The Dual Identity

We believe that our dual sexual identity as male and female emphasizes our need for fellowship and communion. Our dual identity is a call to mutuality and complementarity. Big words, all of them, right? Perhaps an explanation about each of these aspects will make the matter clear.

Opposites Attract

God's wonderful gift of sexual attractiveness is central to communion purposes. He made us in such a way that we are attracted to an opposite identity—the shape and nature of man is desirable to woman, and the shape and nature of woman evokes desires in a man. While we often have misinterpreted these desires as being sinful, they are legitimate, God-given emotions.

God has formed us to desire each other in appropriate ways. Our longing for each other is an aspect of our nature. We wish to commune with an identity not our own; we seek fulfillment and satisfaction of our own nature in such desire. The presence of this attraction inside of us, then, is itself neither sinful nor inappropriate. What becomes inappropriate is the use of these desires in immoral or irresponsible actions. Jesus Christ elevated our understanding even further by emphasizing that sin is more than wrong actions; sin also includes the cultivation of inappropriate and unworthy thoughts (Matt. 5:27-30). Impure actions begin with impure desires.

A third explanation for a dual sexuality refers to the sharing of thought, feeling, and action between two persons of different sexes. This sharing is not the same as the presence or exchange between two persons of the same sex. Such a balancing of personhood is a mutual exchange that adds dimension and depth to each person.

When two such human beings marry, they take on a unique partnership of learning. They have never been so close to another human being of a different sex. They are now in a new encounter with regard to God's other sexual creation. They have become students to a sexual identity different from themselves.

Some marriage partners never seem to understand this distinction. They act as if they know and understand what it is like to be a person of the opposite sex. Some men compare a mother or a sister model to the woman model with whom they are a partner. In the case of a wife, she often will compare the new husband model with the male identities of father and brother. All these models are inadequate and thus produce distortions. The distorted understanding people have of the opposite sex can only be transformed by a relearning process. Let's look at some things each one learns from the other?

Being Male

Several characteristics usually are associated with a man. Aside from the obvious physical differences, our culture and background teach us a lot about what being male means. Some of these ideas are learned at home and some in the community in which we live. Popular interpretations of manhood include being determined, physically aggressive, and emotionally cautious. Men are taught not to display emotions in certain circumstances. Fear, tenderness, pain, and sadness are usually suppressed. Muscular development, assertiveness, and leader-

The concept of being male has grown to include the full range of human emotions.

ship are prized for males, while artistic and homemaking interests are seen with less value.

Being a man today means a great deal more than this general stereotype. The concept of male has grown to include the full range of human emotions. Tenderness and gentleness, as demonstrated by Christ Himself, is slowly returning to characterize men.

At one time, being a male was considered a superior identity. Perhaps the idea was first derived from Old Testament images of men and women. Certainly the Hebrew family had such a notion of male superiority. The Bible, however, steadily challenges and counters this view of man. When God created male and female, He created them for different functions. Neither was given superior position or worth. God is spirit, and His identity is represented in both sexual creatures.

From a biblical point of view, being a man meant being a provider. Yet, the examples of families in the Old and New Testament confirm the fact that women provided as often as men and always worked at least as much as men. The image of a male as a caretaker and responsible leader in the home has prevailed in history. Such leadership at times has been interpreted in oppressive ways.

Paul interpreted the Christian perspective in an age that advocated male superiority. Yet he defined male "headship" as leadership in love (Eph. 5:21-33). He suggested that the male role be one of household leadership, expressed in love. He used the example of Christ's love for the church as our model.

What does it mean, then, to be a man? It means to stand at the center of sexual creation and share God's creative work with a sexual mate. A man is a model of strength, protection, initiative, and nurturing care. He is to be responsible with his mate. He is neither to command nor to impose himself as a tyrant. (Has Christ ever done so with the church?) He is to be first in loving, caring, and supporting his mate.

Being Female

The traditional image of the female sex is that of a more delicate, sensitized partner than the man. Groomed by her culture to see herself as "weaker," she has sometimes thought of herself as inferior. By and large, physically speaking, females are shorter in height, weigh less, and have smaller bone and muscle structure. Women counter their physical stature by developing emotional and physiological stamina.

The female sex has been released by our culture to experience emotions less hindered than men. Women consequently avoid some of the physical and emotional punishment that accompanies inhibited emotional expression. Generally speaking, the female sex is more in touch with feelings than the male.

Girls usually are growing chronologically about three years ahead of boys. Beginning about the third year of life, girls develop emotionally slightly ahead of boys. By the time a girl is 11 or 12, she begins to surge ahead physically. Although boys "catch up" physically in the mid-to-late teens, girls are emotionally more mature than boys until the mid-twenties. This explains the frequent frustration in dating relationships during this stage of life.

What is learned behavior and what is innately "female" is difficult to sort out. From their youngest days, girls seem far more interested in dolls than cars, clothes than sports, and personal care than physical prowess. Fathers and mothers contribute much to these preferences, however; and most of us can immediately think of several exceptions to these general comments.

Stop and Think 29

In what ways should the similarities and differences between male and female determine roles in the marriage relationship?

_____

What do you understand as the primary role of a husband?

_____

What do you understand as the primary role of a wife?

_____

What circumstances could affect roles in the marriage relationship?

_____

Intimacy

The teen years are peak years for sexual interest and physical attraction. As two individuals become interested in each other, the sexual interest and response of both persons also increases. A natural reaction to such added feelings is the attraction to physical contact. Initial intimacies need to take into account the expectations and perceptions of both individuals. Why do we become intimate? What do we intend when we become physically intimate? How do Christians approach physical intimacy responsibly?

The Desire

Individuals may become intimate mainly for physical affection. They seek to feed a desire for physical closeness and warmth. They want to be loved or affirmed physically and emotionally. Their concern in physical affection is not so much to offer affection as to receive it. Much teenage "petting" is concerned with this type of need. The male or female is lonely and seeks to confirm his or her worth and needs in physical gratification. Such needs are appropriate; the problem, however, is that the display of affection may be misleading to the partner. Quite often, lonely individuals overcommunicate care and interest in another person by their intimate actions. What they really want is to be cared for physically; what they tell others with their behavior is that they are more emotionally involved with the partner than they are.

Some individuals explore their sexual curiosity and desire in intimate behavior. They are not concerned mainly in communicating care or interest in the partner. Neither are they concerned about satisfying affection needs. They are motivated by a curiosity about sexual activity. They also are stimulated by the pleasurable sensation of physical intimacy.

The key to appropriate sexual expression is found in a proper understanding of motives. To become physically involved with another person, we must develop both an interest in the person's welfare and a concern for the person's beliefs and feelings. Neither of the two motives mentioned earlier (affection and curiosity) are bad motives. They simply are superficial reasons for an intimate relationship and should not be the primary factor in such closeness.

The Biblical Plan

The biblical plan for communion and closeness is based on a developing oneness. Such gradual blending of two human beings takes place in the context of growing trust, responsibility, and care. Two sexual creatures progress in intimacy as God has planned it when they do so on all levels at the same time. That is, the level of physical intimacy should correspond to the level of commitment. The degree of emotional closeness should go hand in hand with concern and care for the other person. The decision to commune more personally should be based on an understanding of the sacredness of the other human being.

The development of care for one's partner includes an increased understanding of what the person is comfortable with in regard to physical attention. Couples who are growing in emotional interest need to talk about physical intimacy. What is appropriate and what is irresponsible? Because the biblical symbolism of "one flesh" refers to the union of sexual intercourse, such a union should be preserved for the covenant of marriage. Sexual intercourse is the supreme parable of marital unity; its meaning and purpose are accomplished only in the covenant of marriage.

Any sexual exploration that does not preserve sexual union for marriage is cheating the partners of the deepest fulfillment of sexual creation. Human beings were created for sexual intercourse as a full expression of a commitment to unite with another creature of God and to become responsible to that person. An invitation to marriage is an invitation to responsibility, care, and ongoing commitment to another individual. Until persons are prepared to make such commitments, they need to refrain from the corresponding actions that apply to them.

Sexual closeness and physical exploration are begun by a couple voluntarily, and they are maintained or discontinued voluntarily. We are all capable of controlling ourselves. Any actions continued or discontinued are done so by our choosing. Let no one attempt to make anyone or anything else responsible for his or her behavior in sexual exchanges.

━━━━━━━━━━━ Stop and Think 30 ━━━━━━━━━

Why should sexual intercourse be reserved for marriage?

_____

_____

The Assignment of Responsibility

Male and female are responsible together for their actions. The idea that a woman alone should "set the limits" for sexual activity is ridiculous. Men who advocate this nonsense simply lean on an old double standard that is nothing more than avoiding responsibility.

Trust and openness in a relationship help partners know how to set limits for emotional involvement. Here is the place where a man can become a caring student of his female partner, and she of him. What does this mean? Men sometimes do not understand that a woman can become sexually excited in ways different from men. A responsible male partner needs to understand such reactions in order to be a good steward of sexual control.

Men respond to a narrower area of physical contact. Studies reveal that men are stimulated sexually almost entirely in the genital area. Studies also indicate that men achieve sexual intensity more quickly than women but that the male intensity lasts much shorter than the female response. Women respond more gradually in sexual encounters but have sexual

Male and female are responsible together for their actions.

stimulation for a longer period of time. When these facts are ignored by married couples the results are frustration, feelings of rejection, and sexual miscommunication.

Persons who feel close emotionally will naturally desire physical closeness. This closeness may be appropriate and biblically sound up to a point. Decisions about the amount of intimacy are the responsibility of both partners under God. Sexual union is the biblical design for partners who are committed to the care and love of each other—for life!

=============== **Stop and Think 31** ===============

Who is responsible for setting limits of intimacy in a relationship? Why?

_____

What can be done to make sure the relationship stays within the proper limits?

_____

Maturing Love

Individuals who engage in a relationship with mature desire for commitment soon assume an interest in the welfare of their partner. The development of a relationship also means the evolving of respect, responsibility, commitment, and care for each other. From a Christian point of view, the best definition of mature love includes each of these dimensions. Those who love sincerely do so with regard for the other person.

The true strength of God's love in us is the development of an abiding respect. Respect for a partner dictates a reverence for personhood under God. Persons who respect their mates are careful about their attitude, behavior, and feelings around them. They are concerned with the partner's opinions. They are interested in the person's feelings. They are influenced by the other person's viewpoint.

Value placed on a partner also shapes responses to the person. Loving partners seek the welfare and interest of the other person. How both feel, what they believe, and how they want to act is of importance to each one. Sexual love assumes the value of the other person as a human being created for God's purposes. Regard for another means that the mate's needs and feelings may take preference over one's own; mature love gives way at times out of respect and admiration for the other person.

Responsibility is another dimension of mature love. People who love deeply cultivate the decision to assume responsibility for the relationship. This does not imply that marital vows mean taking over someone else's life; it does mean that the bond being established includes a desire to become responsive to the other person's needs. The one flesh concept takes shape when two individuals decide to answer life's challenges together. Individuals are choosing to become attached to and a part of someone else's life.

Commitment is a third essential ingredient in the love being described. Unlike the unpredictable secular variety of love that is based on feelings, this love is based on will. Mature love is a calculated decision to become invested in another person's life—for keeps. "Covenant" is the biblical term for this commitment. Partners who learn to care for each other develop a consistent desire to remain faithful to the relationship.

The ability to care for someone else is the gradual nurturing of feelings and thoughts until a particular person is valued to us. One first sign of this development is the pain that occurs when the relationship is threatened. We may hurt when someone is absent (whom we miss); we may hurt when someone misunderstands us (from whom we feel apart); or we may hurt when someone leaves us (from whom we feel alienated). On the other hand, the pleasure and excitement of the person's presence is a sure sign that we care for that one!

These caring qualities are crucial. We affirm and support the sexual identity of a partner by our respect, responsibility, commitment, and care of that person. We are co-partners with the person for God's creative work. We are, therefore, stewards of all that enriches the experience of oneness. We offer trust, concern, dignity, and respect to our partner. Those same gifts are offered back to us in an atmosphere of security and encouragement.

We regard our mates as the temple of the Holy Spirit. The care, responsibility, commitment, and respect offered to God's sanctuary is the same offered to our mate. The development of our partnership will only be enhanced if we keep that goal in mind as we relate to each other.

Caring for each other involves the continuing interest in physical, emotional, and spiritual welfare. The total person is steadily considered. A mate will constantly bear in mind what is healthful and good for the partner. A medical exam from time to time is one way of ensuring that both persons are properly cared for. Interest in each other's physical condition is a supportive gesture.

Concern for the emotional welfare of a partner is also important. To be able to share from the values and concerns that shape us is a vital link in the process of becoming united as a couple. Time spent on spiritual and emotional union provides the foundation for a stable sexual union.

Stop and Think 32

Explain how each of the following elements should be lived out in a dating relationship as preparation for a marriage relationship.

Respect _____

Responsibility _____

Commitment _____

Care _____

May the God of perspective and wisdom guide us as we tenderly respect and employ the wonderful and powerful expression of our sexual identities!

WHAT AM I TO DO? AND YOU?

*W*e all have enjoyed watching children at play, pretending to be the "doctor" tending a "sick baby," the "fireman" zooming through the streets with "siren" wailing, the "spaceman" conquering an army of "foreign invaders." Children are extremely curious about roles and eager to grow up to become whatever interests them most. The games are fascinating and important in their stage of development; but, as they grow older, the games give way to pressing dilemmas.

Childhood dreams, limited only by the imagination, fade in the realities of commitment, maturity, and responsibility. Anxiety develops. Why does this happen? Are we threatened by the realization that a definite choice will limit our once-abundant freedom? Are we frightened by the face-to-face encounter with daily responsibility? Are we hesitant to face the consequences that a career choice brings? Whatever the reasons, anxieties affect our understanding of the adventure that lies ahead.

Approaching the Adventure

Basically, there are two approaches to life. You can live life, or you can let life live you. Perhaps the words *technique* and *purpose* present the idea better.

Technique.—Living by technique is simply trying to "get by." This approach involves an effort to do just enough to make it through. Some people want to learn or do as little as possible to get the quickest results. The better the technique they have, the quicker they will reach their goals. A few examples illustrate this point. The first is the education route.

Education has become a technique for getting a degree and, thereby, obtaining a job. For this reason high schools and colleges are packed with students who are concerned more with the grades they'll make than the subject or lessons they learn. When students major on mastering shortcuts to good exam grades, they miss the more important lessons of the daily classroom experience.

Developing the idea further, a job may simply become a technique for making money. Making money is not wrong in itself, but it becomes a poor substitute for the joy and pride of accomplishment that give meaning to daily work. Many adults have bought into this technique-oriented approach to work and are bogged down in a no-win situation with their jobs. The only fulfillment they feel comes at the end of each pay period. That paycheck, however, can be small compensation for the investment of time and energy.

Living by technique is not limited to the educational or vocational area of life; it saturates the relational side as well. If we choose friends by technique, they are chosen for what they can do for us rather than for who they are. Choosing a marriage partner by technique can become an even more devastating expression of "relational usefulness." Seeing the partner in terms of physical beauty, social status, material possessions, or talent could become a technique for a self-beneficial marriage.

Purpose.—While living by technique can be a shallow and hollow approach to life, living with purpose is to live in the dimension of the soul. Theologians call this "understanding one's sense of calling." In this approach, education is seen not just as preparation for the job market but rather as preparation for all of life. Life is a continuous learning process, growth that is nurtured by previous experiences.

Living with purpose measures a job's value by the amount of fulfillment that comes from using one's gifts and talents for a worthwhile purpose rather than solely in terms of salary. Relationships also thrive with such purpose because growth, intimacy, and compassion become the goals of marriage and friendship rather than mere by-products.

Considering Techniques vs. Purpose

The problem of technique versus purpose is not new. It has been here since people began to interact with one another. This problem is a constant theme in the life and teachings of Jesus. Over and over again Jesus challenged the scribes and Pharisees to evaluate their pattern for living and move from lives centered on learning the techniques of Godlike living to learning the purpose for Godlike living.

A classic example of the technique versus purpose dilemma is found in Jesus' encounter with the rich young ruler: "And as

He was setting out on a journey, a man ran up to Him and knelt before Him, and began asking Him, 'Good Teacher, what shall I do to inherit eternal life?' And Jesus said to him, 'Why do you call Me good? No one is good except God alone. You know the commandments, 'Do not murder, Do not commit adultery, Do not steal, Do not bear false witness, Do not defraud, Honor your Father and Mother.' And he said to Him, 'Teacher, I have kept all these things from my youth up.' And looking at him, Jesus felt a love for him, and said to him, 'One thing you lack: go and sell all you possess, and give to the poor, and you shall have treasure in heaven; and come, follow Me.' But at these words his face fell, and he went away grieved, for he was one who owned much property" (Mark 10:17-22).

What we see in this passage is a man who had mastered the

Living with purpose measures a job's value by the amount of fulfillment that comes from using one's gifts and talents.

techniques demanded for a godly life but who did not understand the purpose for a godly life. We see an individual who had learned how to get inside the law of the universe. He was skilled at not violating specific laws, but he had little understanding of the spirit or the essence of the law. Jesus tried to move the young man from negative techniques to a positive purpose for life. Abundant living is not found in avoiding the perils of life but rather in facing them and attempting to solve them.

The struggle to find purpose in life is an age-old undertaking. One of the curious ironies that we cannot seem to grasp is the fact that we have never been nor will ever be able to achieve enough techniques to get by.

Consider the history of our world's knowledge and techniques as condensed by Alvin Toffler in his book *Future Shock:* "Only during the last seventy lifetimes has it been possible to communicate effectively from one lifetime to another—as writing made it possible to do. Only during the last six lifetimes did masses of men ever see a printed word. Only during the last four has it been possible to measure time with any precision. Only in the last two has anyone, anywhere used an electric motor. And the overwhelming majority of all the material goods we use in daily life today have been developed within the present . . . lifetime."[1] What Toffler was alluding to is the fact that the rate of knowledge development and invention is getting faster and faster. His premise is that it is now impossible to keep up with the growing technological knowledge.

Even if we were able to know everything about everything today, in 10 years we would know only half of all there is to know! What is astounding is that the inventions and discoveries that are being made today will drastically alter our lives in the years to come. People who are studying in one specific area today may find their field obsolete by the time they are ready to take their places in that field. This means that we are facing the distinct possibility of multiple careers. We may have to train for several different jobs in the future. This, as well as the biblical imperative, seems to shout to us: "Discover the purpose for your life and then live out that purpose wherever and whatever your job may be."

===
============== **Stop and Think 33** ==============
===

Explain in your own words the difference between approaching life from a technique point of view and a purpose point of view.

_____

_____

Determining God's Will

What does God want with me? What is His calling for my life? In order to get proper answers for those questions, we must evaluate our understanding of God and His nature. How we see God plays a large part in how we relate to Him.

Some see God as a "cosmic policeman" who is constantly keeping track of our actions. This kind of God instills fear in His people, and the relationship between the two is a monologue. He speaks and we listen. He commands and we obey or face stern punishment.

Others see God as a senile, old grandfather-type whose purpose is merely to make us happy. This kind of God is around only at certain times and spends most of that time spoiling us and fulfilling our wants and desires. This type of relationship is also one-sided, but this time it is we who speak and expect God to listen.

Neither of these understandings of God is biblical. The God of the Bible comes to us as Father, one who is in control but, at the same time, deeply desires a loving relationship with His children. Our Creator is neither an uncompromising tyrant nor a doting grandfather. He is Lord!

When we begin to see God's fatherly characteristics of love and justice, we gain a new understanding of our places in the world. God's will is that we be the best persons we can be. If we are responsible enough to accept the innate talents and abilities He has given us and realize that we do not need more or less of them to become the person He would have us be, we see more clearly God's purpose for us and our world.

Sometimes it is easier to look back and see how God has dealt with us, given us encouragement, and strengthened our faith. We must ask ourselves these questions: What are the significant faith experiences in my past? What experiences have fashioned who I am today? What individuals have given me direction in discovering who I am? Taking periodic journeys into the past to reexamine those events that have shaped our life journey helps us to give thanks for God's presence in times of frustration and testing. Present burdens and cares seem less overwhelming. We know that God is working out His purposes in us. We are not finished creatures. We are still in process.

Stop and Think 34

Scan the preceding section to select a sentence that expresses what God wants for all His children. Circle the sentence; then write the sentence on the line below.

_____

Answer the following questions to review how God has dealt with you in the past.

_____

What experiences have fashioned who you are today?

_____

What are some significant faith experiences in your past?

_____

What individuals have given you direction in discovering who you are?

_____

What do these experiences say about your future?

_____

God is vitally involved with us. He shares in the joy of our victories and in the depression of our defeats. Most of all God encourages us; He calls us forward. So, just as it is important for us to look at our past, it is also important to take inventory of our present.

Discovering and Using Gifts and Abilities

A great joy in understanding God's involvement with us is the realization that He created us as unique individuals. He desperately wants us to discover our uniqueness, our identity. When that happens our lives assume their potential for service in His kingdom. We don't have to search the world over looking for our calling; it is right here with us. God created us to be what we are, with gifts in some areas and not in others.

One clue to discovering God's purpose in our lives is to identify those things that make us genuinely happy, fully human. The problem is that we spend most of our time comparing our gifts and abilities with others. When we do this we come away dissatisfied, because there is always someone who seems more talented and competent. Ironically, we forget that another person's gifts might not have made us happy in the first place. Jesus saw this problem two thousand years ago and addressed it through a story.

"Now after a long time the master of those servants came and settled accounts with them. And he who had received the five talents came forward, bringing five talents more, saying, 'Master, you delivered to me five talents; here I have made five talents more.' His master said to him, 'Well done, good and faithful servant; you have been faithful over a little, I will set you over much; enter into the joy of your master.' And he also who had the two talents came forward, saying, 'Master, you delivered to me two talents; here I have made two talents more.' His master said to him, 'Well done, good and faithful servant; you have been faithful over a little, I will set you over much; enter into the joy of your master.' He also who had received the one talent came forward, saying, 'Master, I knew you to be a hard

God expects us to use our gifts.

man, reaping where you did not sow, and gathering where you did not winnow; so I was afraid, and I went and hid your talent in the ground. Here you have what is yours.' But his master answered him, 'You wicked and slothful servant! You knew that I reap where I have not sowed, and gather where I have not winnowed? Then you ought to have invested my money with the bankers, and at my coming I should have received what was my own with interest'" (Matt. 25:19-27).

Many of us picture ourselves as that one-talent individual. At times we are so frustrated and angry about our seeming lack of abilities that we don't do anything but sulk. Maybe it's because we are afraid that, if we do try anything, we will fail. At any rate, we may become so resentful that we can't see any good in our lives and are jealous of the good we see in others. Our enthusiasm for life is missing. We are content with the status quo, because the status quo won't demand anything of us. Woe to anyone who tries to budge us from our comfortable position. We have great excuses for our inactivity.

The parable of the talents deserves a closer inspection than merely to focus on the one-talent servant. The key to Jesus' lesson may possibly lie in the reaction of the other two servants, the gifted ones. One significant detail is the master's response to both of their efforts. It was the same. "Well done, thou good and faithful servant," He said to both of them. What mattered to the master was not the total amount accumulated but rather the effort that was made. What would have happened if, in a worthwhile venture, one of those two servants had lost all the talents he had been given? Our hunch is that the master would have applauded his efforts. He would have blessed intention and purpose and forgiven the results and technique.

One curious side note about this story remains—those of us who see ourselves as 10-talent persons must realize that these gifts are given for service. In other words, those who have received much, much will be required (see Luke 12:48).

Stop and Think 35

What have you done to discover and use your gifts?

_____

_____

In what ways do you take advantage of opportunities to use your gifts?

_____

_____

_____

Pray that God will guide you in discovering and using your gifts.

A helpful gift-discovery book is *How to Discover Your Spiritual Gifts*. Order from Customer Service Center, 127 Ninth Ave., North, Nashville, TN 37234, or call 1-800-458-BSSB.

Heeding the Call

How does all of this relate to vocation? We have inspected where we've been and what we feel we have to work with. More important, we have realized a sense of worth—"what we are" is an expression of "who and whose we are!" We should be ready to improve and refine our gifts and use them to the best of our abilities. God is eager to lend us His guidance.

A favorite childhood Bible story relates Samuel's experience in the Temple (1 Sam. 3:1-10). Samuel was in the Temple, living under the guardianship of Eli. One evening, as they were both in bed, Samuel heard a voice calling to him. He thought it was Eli. He immediately interrupted Eli's slumber to "answer" him. After several of these interruptions, Eli realized that the Lord was calling Samuel, and he wisely told Samuel to respond in reverent awareness. The Lord then gave Samuel his first instructions at living out his calling.

Two things are important in Samuel's story. The first is the realization that God speaks to us in ways that we may not recognize. The second significant awareness is that God sends us an Eli to help us understand our calling; we are not alone in this venture.

As we pursue God's will for our lives, we need to be aware that, in His love, He has given us gifts that can bring meaning to our lives. In His justice He holds us responsible for evaluating, nurturing, and using these gifts. Our options are many. Through sensitivity to God's guidance, we can make vocational choices according to His plan for us.

Relating Vocation to Choosing a Marriage Partner

Vocation obviously is one of the most important factors considered by an individual in choosing a marriage partner. What an individual plans to do with his or her life affects what that person's spouse will do. Determining purpose or calling is difficult enough for one person, but combining the plans of two separate people is a constant struggle. Thus, in the choosing of a partner as well as the marriage itself, there is the need for continual communication, understanding, and discovery. If marriage is to be a covenant relationship, it will be governed by understanding and flexibility, not by hard-and-fast rules or regulations. It will be geared to "faithing" life with each other, in spite of the difficult situations that come along.

A covenant relationship must provide for freedom to grow. Humpty Dumpty made a beautiful statement about this kind of freedom in marriage as he jousted with Alice about her understanding of growth.

> "I never ask advice about growing," Alice said indignantly.
>
> "Too proud?" Humpty Dumpty inquired.
>
> Alice felt even more indignant at this suggestion. "I mean," she said, "that one cannot help growing older."
>
> "One can't, perhaps," said Humpty Dumpty, "but two can."[2]

There you have it. One cannot help growing old, but two can. Marriage is growing together through life rather than merely growing old!

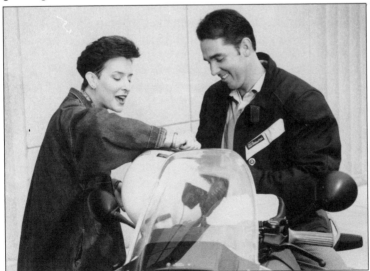

Marriage partners should bring out the best in each other.

When thinking about a person to share this kind of future, one should choose an individual who has the potential to become a best friend for life. This type of person brings out the best in a partner at each juncture of life. This person should be one who is committed to stand by the other in all circumstances, to speak the words of grace and forgiveness as needed, to speak words of justice when an individual has gone astray, to give the words of love that transcend any situation. This person also should be able to stand apart. Of utmost importance is the need for each person to accept the other's individuality. Thus, there is the responsibility to be sensitive and caring, to strive not for control but to seek understanding. Kahlil Gibran defined such a relationship:

> Let there be space in your togetherness,
> and let the winds of heaven dance
> between you.
> Love one another, but make not a bond
> of love . . .
> Even as the strings of a lute are alone
> though they quiver with the same music.
> Give your hearts, but not into each
> other's keeping . . .
> For the pillars of the temple stand apart,
> And the oak tree and the cypress grow
> not in each other's shadow.[3]

The depth of such a relationship cannot be developed instantly but takes time and effort to achieve. It is important to find a person who encourages variety, learning new things about oneself and discovering in the process of everyday life the exciting, unexpected element that inspires a person to new realms of possibilities.

Also, it is important to find a person with whom one can communicate. Contemporary dating situations keep us entertained at movies, concerts, and sports events, but fail to provide settings that develop communication skills. It is crucial to be able to talk to one's partner about things that matter most and to know that he or she is just as concerned about those fears-feelings-dreams.

Vocation should be kept in perspective as two persons choose to marry. We don't choose a person because of his or her vocation. We don't view vocational choice as being a fixed element; still, a spouse who is happy and fulfilled in his or her work and is actively seeking to live out God's purpose for life will be a better marriage partner.

Maintaining an atmosphere of communication, flexibility, and growth is not easy. But dedication to and awareness of God's guidance as a couple will foster intimacy and strength. To follow God's calling means that we see vocational choice, not as an anchor that holds us to one fixed point, but rather as a compass by which we pass through the uncharted waters of our lives. Thus, the pursuit of God's purpose and calling is centered on the God who has come to show us the way.

Stop and Think 36

What does God's call mean to you?

_____

How would your sense of call be fulfilled if you were married?

_____

What are some vocational choices in which you could use your gifts?

_____

---

[1]Alvin Toffler, *Future Shock* (New York: Random House, 1970), pp. 13-14.
[2]Lewis Carroll, *Through the Looking Glass* (New York: Random House, 1946), p. 91.
[3]Kahlil Gibran, *The Prophet* (New York: Alfred A. Knopf, 1957), pp. 16-17. Used by permission.

WHAT IS MY FAMILY LIKE? WHAT WILL MY NEW FAMILY BE?

*T*he families we were born into are the source of much love. The family new partners form is the source of much excitement. And the family new mates plan is the source of much hope. Each of these aspects of family life make significant contributions to life together. In this chapter we will examine issues that affect how we manage each of these areas of our lives.

Families and Independence

We have learned how to think, feel, and act largely through the families in which we grew up. When we begin to move away from our family and consider the formation of a new family, we probably start by moving away physically, either to go to school or to start work. Whether or not we have left our family physically by the time we reach our late teens and early twenties, we begin to see ourselves as adults. Hopefully, other family members will see us that way, too.

Early preparation for leaving one's home of the past includes the ability to think and act like an adult. We gradually bridge the link between adolescence and adulthood as we slowly "earn" the right to be considered an adult. Financial independence plays an important part in this development. Evidence indicates that parents and young adults both view the emerging adult as being more mature if the person is financially independent.

Stop and Think 37

What do you think individuals need to do to "earn" their right to be treated as an adult?

_____

_____

Why should marriage be for adults only?

_____

Parents sometimes hold on to their grown children, encouraging them to be dependent. And some young people, who do not wish to leave the "nest" encourage the continuation of parenting. For these and other reasons, young adults may find it difficult to pull away from their family of origin. But, by the late teens, most persons are ready to declare physical and emotional independence from their parents. We conveniently postpone financial independence until the early twenties.

Shifting Loyalties

When two persons become interested in marriage, the issue of independence from childhood families needs to be discussed. Some young adults are quite emotionally attached to their parents and are not prepared to shift their emotional attention to a new family. Other young adults have created such distance from their families that they are isolated. A healthy balance in family relationships takes into account the need for distance from parental families. However, excessive distance and lack of contact creates tension and awkwardness with which both new partners must cope. The young person who maintains and develops a proper adult relationship with parents before marriage is doing much toward making a smooth transition to a marriage partner.

Young people should naturally consult and share with loved ones. However, adults who continue to rely on parental authority over and against the word of a spouse are hindering the establishment of a new family. Young men and women who marry need to rely on their mate as the first source of opinion and authority.

There is no one pattern to the process of letting go of parents. Although a frequent stress is that of a male partner's relationship to his mother, other transitions often occur. The father who has always treated his daughter as his "little girl" will strain to adjust to a new male in her life. If the daughter herself has accepted that role, she may have difficulty accepting her mate's opinion over that of her dad. The issues and persons may vary, but the key question is almost always one of possessiveness for the parents and maturity for the grown children.

Possessiveness refers to a parent's need to hold on to the child's dependent relationship. A sound and healthy parent-adult relationship can be enriching and meaningful, but some parents have an unhealthy need to retain a relationship of control over their grown son or daughter. Probably there is no greater threat to the future of a young marriage than the constant attempt by a parent to direct the course of a couple's life.

Some persons find it necessary to move geographically away from their parents in order to gain the needed independence. The problem is often twofold; not only does one mate resist "letting go" of parental domination, but parents also encourage dependence. Until the young adult takes action to gain emotional independence, the transition to adult status has not been completed.

Stop and Think 38

Read Genesis 2:24: "For this cause a man shall leave his father and his mother, and shall cleave to his wife; and they shall become one flesh."

Study this verse in a commentary. Also talk to your pastor or youth leader about the meaning of the one-flesh concept. Summarize the results of your study by answering the following questions.

What is the meaning of the one-flesh concept?

_____

What are some ways this concept is lived out in the marriage relationship?

_____

_____

Young men and women certainly do not stop loving their parents when they prepare for marriage. Rather, they begin a deliberate process of shifting loyalties and first allegiances to the one with whom they have chosen to spend life. Such a transition takes time; it should, however, progress steadily. A sound, secure marriage is built when two persons turn toward each other for emotional support, strength, and direction, rather than to their parents.

Meeting Prospective In-laws

Persons who begin serious conversations about marriage rarely think that their family will not be accepted. Yet the fact that we love our family of origin is no guarantee that they are lovable to others. Neither is the fact that we are attracted to someone any indication that the person's family members will also be attractive to us. Potential marriage candidates need to know that acceptance depends on a number of factors.

Stanley and Jill had been dating for several months, and their feelings for each other had grown steadily. When Stanley told Jill that his family would be in town, she was anxious to meet them. The nearer the day came for the introduction, the more excited Jill became. She was extremely disappointed when her enthusiasm was squelched by a very casual greeting from Stanley's parents. Jill didn't know it, but their reaction was due to the fact that, in the past, Stanley had introduced them to many "fine" girls.

So many first encounters between "chosen" mates and their prospective in-laws are disappointing. The selected partner is anxious to please and to be accepted. The parents are cautious in their response. Each is assessing the other. Young men and women need to remember that a meaningful relationship is built over a period of time. Men and women also need to know that they can help in the beginning phases of this parent-marriage partner encounter. So, what can we do to ease the process of relating to the family of our mate?

One thing we can do is to prepare a potential mate for a first meeting. We become "ministers of introduction" when we assist our chosen partner and our parents in effectively meeting the newness of this relationship. We can do this by "explaining" our family to our future mate. Each family has a set of individuals with particular quirks that can be explained and interpreted. A newcomer in any family group can be assisted greatly by knowing the background of each person. A conversation that interprets a family fairly to an interested partner can be redemptive and helpful.

A second effort toward effective in-law introductions is the choosing of a good setting for such a meeting. Persons who are in the business of meeting new people and making them feel at home tell us that meals are ideal occasions for first meetings. The Bible is full of examples of meetings scheduled as fellowship meals (see Mark 2:16; 14:12-15; Acts 2:46). This kind of atmosphere helps to assure a positive initial encounter between strangers. The pleasant activity of sharing food can be a buffer in the process of anxious introductory moments.

A non-threatening agenda helps "mate-meet-parents" occasions.

First encounters between potential family members can be structured for brief conversations. Long introductory meetings may fatigue all those involved. A wise planner limits encounters so that all persons leave with a desire for additional time together. It is far better to wish we had more time with individuals than to wish we had not spent so long with them. Sometimes a first meeting between parents and marrying partners occurs on the occasion of a wedding rehearsal. Those who can plan differently should consider a less-pressured occasion for such beginnings. Most persons who are involved in wedding rehearsals have traveled a long time and usually are exhausted.

Having a positive non-threatening agenda helps "mate-meet-parents" sessions. If the two partners can spend a few minutes planning a series of constructive, pleasant topics (related to the family), an introductory time will be more effective. Controversial subjects or issues are rarely effective content for beginning moments in a conversation. A few favorite starters are: Tell me about yourselves. Where were you born, and where did you grow up? Tell me a little more about your family. What are the qualities you appreciate most about your daughter (or son)? The more individuals talk about familiar topics, the more comfortable they feel.

Young people can benefit from knowing where others are in their relationship to their own family. If time is spent interpreting issues and aspects of our own experience with our parents, the partner will better know how to respond to our parents. Often, young adults are moving through certain issues in the family relationship. A partner who is informed about the particular issues can more effectively cooperate in establishing harmonious dialogue.

These and other matters need evaluation by persons considering marriage. When counseling with potential marriage partners, I ask them to discuss which family members they are closest to and which one they feel is the most difficult to understand. Some other possible questions are: Who do you think will be the most difficult person to get along with in your partner's family? How can the partner help you with that person?

Although young people often are struggling with their own relationship to parents, they all want their partner to like their family. We do not outgrow our need for our families of nurture. We will grieve if marriage creates distance between us and our loved ones; and we will rejoice if our potential mate devotes energy and interest toward accepting our parents and family.

Stop and Think 39

Develop a dialog for a first meeting between you and prospective in-laws. Write your thoughts here.

_____

_____

Loving In-laws

Understanding the nature of grief associated with loss will assist persons in accepting their in-laws. For at least eighteen years, these parents cared for the person they must share with a marriage partner. They gave that individual all they know and are and now will experience permanent distance from them. They remember well that they left their own parents and that it was a brand new venture. If individuals can realize that much of the in-laws' resistance actually is a process of letting go slowly, then they may begin to love them in their loss. Not that "holding on" is appropriate—they and we know it is time to let go. The business of releasing, however, is more complex than simply declaring that it will be so and that it is right.

Another step in learning to love the "inherited family" is taking the time to get to know them. Most forms of prejudice are related to lack of information and lack of exposure. If couples plan occasions in which they spend time seeking to know and understand these new people in their lives, they will be rewarded. The immediate reward is the joy that someone is interested in them; the long-term gain is a potentially solid friendship. To know in-laws well usually is to love them.

Time—a patient transition that allows parents of a future mate to get accustomed to his or her new plans—is an added gift. Couples who plan their marriage to include "acceptance" time for their parents will gain allies. Everyone needs time to adjust to major events. The chance to learn and to adjust together may be one of the most bonding ventures in which couples and their parents may participate. In-law loving is a gradual, surprising development. As time goes by, couples surprise themselves with how much they have come to care for their in-laws.

Stop and Think 40

Talk to an older married couple who has developed a good relationship with their in-laws over the years. Ask them the following questions. Record answers in the space provided.

What was your most difficult adjustment in becoming part of your spouse's family?

_____

What are some things you did to get to know and understand your in-laws?

_____

_____

_____

What would you do differently if you had the get-acquainted time to go through all over again?

_____

What would you do the same if you had the get-acquainted time to go through all over again?

_____

Planning a Family

A normal question for any possible candidate for marriage is whether the person wants children. Some young couples today question parenthood as a calling for them. Many are determining the proper time for an addition to their family. Both issues are central to Christian parenting.

The assumption that God calls all married people to parenthood is easily challenged. We do not believe that God has called every couple to nurture children of their own. Some people, by virtue of their vocational call and commitment, lead a life-style that is not suitable to responsible parenting. Some people are unable to have children and transform a beautiful yearning for parenting into a ministry with persons who do not live with their biological parents.

Both potential mates should openly discuss their feelings about being parents. Hidden feelings can cause a major frustration and obstacle in the marriage covenant. Too often young people enter parenthood by accident. Some young couples take on parenting quite casually and bring into the world children they never intend to adequately care for. Therefore, the first question that a potential marriage partner should answer is not how many children he or she wants but whether God has called him or her to parenthood. This idea of an option about parenting is surprising to some young people. But failure to consider parenting as an option may lead to poor commitment to parenting.

Some young adults need time to decide the issue of parenting. The decision requires prayerful evaluation. A majority of marriage candidates who decide that they will not have children change their minds in the first seven years of marriage. For that reason, couples who discuss the issue should allow flexibility in their responses. They also should plan to review the question frequently. Some of the initial fears of having children and bringing them up eventually disappear. Other serious issues do not; that is why the question about parenting is so personal.

Often, young people are forced to face the issues of parenting long before they come to terms with their own identities.

They may fear children because they are not sure about themselves. Others are asked about parenting before they know their vocational commitments. Naturally, people who do not understand themselves and who do not know where they are headed would fear adding new responsibilities to their uncertain future. Such hesitation needs to be received with sensitivity.

When a couple decides to have children, it is important to consider God's direction for their children's lives. Discussions about children should include how soon the couple plans to start a family, how many children they want to have, and their expectations for sons or daughters. They need to share their hopes with each other. Sharing expectations about children is vital for good communication and support.

Couples who have major educational or financial chal-

The calling of parenthood involves an ongoing responsibility and faithfulness.

lenges to face need to consider carefully the introduction of children into their home. Although some people still advocate having children "as they occur," most Christian young people understand that their choosing and planning of a family is in keeping with God's careful plans and order in creation. Certainly the God of the Bible is a God who plans all things in their season and time. He also is a God who declares responsible stewardship by the way He orders and determines creation. As His stewards, we have good cause to believe that planning how we will add to our family is both biblical and responsible.

Couples need to discuss their personal beliefs about birth control. They should be frank and sensitive at this point, because feelings usually are signals to deeper beliefs. Respecting and discussing different points of view is critical for the trust and welfare of two potential marriage mates. The subject deserves the best communication. Avoiding the issue is a poor show of modesty.

Several responsible methods of birth control are available. A doctor is the best source for such information. A pastor may also be helpful. The assumption that a woman should be the controlling mate is unfounded. Couples should discuss together what approach is best in keeping with their beliefs and physical circumstances.

Too many young parents assume that their commitment to children is mainly for food, clothing, shelter, and love. The Christian parent understands that parenthood is a calling to provide the guidance and nurture that the Bible declares is God's way of bringing children into the world. Adults who decide to become parents do so with a determination to provide daily for their children's emotional needs. They also assume the joyful and dangerous opportunity of providing for them spiritually. However, a large percentage of male parents ignore the responsibility for the spiritual nurture of their offspring. More children are taken to church and taught beliefs by the mother than at any time in history. Fathers need to recover the biblical role of a spiritual leader who provides the daily care and admonition of a loving, responsible parent.

Stop and Think 41

Contemplate your future by answering the following questions.

Do you plan to have children? If so, how many?

_____

_____

After marriage, how long do you want to wait before starting a family? Give reasons for your answer.

_____

What kind of birth control do you plan to use?

_____

_____

What plans do you have for the religious training of your children?

_____

If you are considering marriage in the near future, discuss these questions with your prospective mate. Otherwise, share your answers with a friend and save your answers to share with your prospective mate in the future.

In this book, we have raised an important cross section of central concerns about Christian marriage. Each chapter was designed to introduce a subject related to marriage, not exhaust it. Hopefully, each of the sections has evoked a thirst for further investigation and dialog on Christian marriage. May the God of beautiful purposes be with you as you consider His plan and calling for you in the future!

Group Learning Activities

The Group Learning Activities are designed to secure active involvement of youth in the study of *Before You Marry.* Many of the activities have been developed with the assumption that the youth have read the study material in each chapter and have completed the Stop and Think activities before the session. If this is not practical for your situation, allow time for youth to complete the activities during the session. Feel free to adapt the suggestions for the eight, one-hour sessions to the needs of your group.

Secure copies of *Before You Marry* well in advance of the time scheduled for the study. Carefully study the book and complete the Stop and Think activities in each chapter. Plan to distribute the book prior to the first session. For each session each youth will need a copy of the book, a Bible, and a pencil.

Pray that group members will gain an understanding of the purpose of marriage and will learn what is involved in making an enduring commitment to a marriage partner.

Session 1
Why Should I Marry?

Session Goals: Youth will (1) identify God's purposes for marriage, (2) summarize the meaning of concepts related to marriage, and (3) identify the basic purposes for marriage.

AGENDA

1. Consider the Purposes for Marriage (5 Min.)
2. Hear from the "Experts" (25)
3. Summarize Marriage Concepts (20)
4. Compare Answers (10)

Before the Session

☐ Distribute books to members. Assign chapter 1. Suggest that youth complete the Stop and Think activities before the session.

☐ Study chapter 1 and the Introduction and complete the Stop and Think activities.

☐ Enlist three married, Christian couples to serve as panel members. Try to choose a newly married couple, a middle-aged couple, and an older couple. Ask that they prepare answers to the following questions to present to the group: (1) How and why did you decide to marry? Was there a formal proposal? (2) How have your ideas about marriage changed and modified over the years? (3) What advice would you give about how to conduct oneself on a date? (4) What guidance and advice would you give to someone contemplating marriage? (5) How is marriage a partnership? Ask each couple to limit their remarks to five minutes.

☐ Prepare copies of the following assignment for group work:

1. Refer to the section that includes your assigned word.
2. Summarize the meaning of the word as it relates to marriage.

☐ Have available paper, pencils, extra copies of *Before You Marry*, and Bibles for those who did not bring one.

During the Session

1. Consider the Purposes for Marriage
• As members arrive, give each one a pencil and ask them to complete Stop and Think 1 (from now on we will refer to these exercises as ST). When it is time to begin, inform the group that you will discuss answers at the end of the session.

2. Hear from the "Experts"
• Introduce the panel members. Distribute paper and encourage the youth to take notes as the panel members share information. When they are finished allow time for questions.

3. Summarize Marriage Concepts
• Form small groups. Assign the following words to the

groups (depending on the size of your group, you may need to assign more than one word to a small group): *dependence, responsibility, fidelity, parenting, fellowship, love, vulnerability, covenant.* Give each group a copy of the directions that were prepared before the session. For their summary of the meaning of the assigned word as it relates to marriage, you could suggest that they select sentences from the section to summarize the meaning of the word or that they write their own summary.

When the groups have completed the assignment, call for reports. Use these suggestions to follow up on some of the reports: (1) After the report on *dependence*, guide the group in completing ST 2. Record on the chalkboard the number of yes and no answers. Also record a list of advantages and disadvantages of the married and single life-styles that members name. (2) After the report on *fidelity*, guide the group in completing ST 3. (3) After the report on *love*, guide the group in completing ST 4. (4) After the report on *vulnerability*, ask for someone who completed ST 5 to share what they wrote.

4. Compare Answers
• Ask members to complete ST 6. Ask volunteers to share what they wrote. Lead the group to agree on the three most important purposes for marriage. Then have members share what they wrote for the final question in ST 6.

Pray that each person will gain a deeper understanding of marriage as a result of this study.

Assign chapter 2 for the next session. Encourage youth to complete the ST exercises before the session.

Session 2
What Do I Expect of Marriage?

Session Goals: Youth will (1) share expectations for marriage, (2) illustrate marriage expectations, (3) examine false and true expectations for marriage, (4) tell how Matthew 19:4-6 emphasizes the permanence of marriage, and (5) revise marriage expectations.

AGENDA

1. Share Expectations (5 Min.)
2. Picture Expectations (15)
3. Determine False Expectations (15)
4. Explore True Expectations (15)

Before the Session
☐ Study chapter 2 and complete the Stop and Think activities.
☐ Secure the following materials for preparing collages: magazines that contain advertisements and pictures related to society's concept of the ideal marriage; several large pieces of poster board, paste or tape, and magic markers.
☐ Prepare a minilecture on the section "True Words." Record the four truths on the chalkboard or a large piece of white paper. Also do commentary study on Matthew 19:4-6.
☐ Enlist two youth to be prepared to share the results of an interview with an older couple as suggested in ST 12.
☐ Have available pencils, paper, study books, and Bibles.

During the Session
1. Share Expectations
• Ask volunteers to share answers to the question in ST 7 (allow time for them to write answers to the question, if necessary). Record answers on the chalkboard.
2. Picture Expectations
• Form pairs. Distribute materials for making collages. Direct

them to tear out pictures and ads that illustrate popular ideas about an ideal marriage. Also suggest that they write statements or draw pictures to illustrate their concept of an ideal marriage. After allowing about 10 minutes for the pairs to develop collages, call for reports. Ask each pair to briefly interpret their collage. Display each collage on a focal wall. Keep these collages for use in session 6.

3. Determine False Expectations

• When the collages have been interpreted, ask, What false expectations are illustrated in these collages? (If the group does not respond quickly, suggest that they scan the section "False Expectations" for ideas.) List responses on the chalkboard.

• Use these suggestions to discuss the false expectations: For "False Idea 1" have someone read the example in this section, beginning with "Did you see that new guy." Ask, Why is that not love? For "False Idea 2" guide the group in completing and discussing ST 8. For "False Idea 3" discuss ST 9. For "False Idea 4" have the group silently read about Joe and Linda. Ask, How does their experience show that you can't live on love alone? Briefly touch on "False Idea 5" and note that you will discuss communication techniques in the next session. For "False Idea 6" ask members to express how much of a problem they think this is.

4. Explore True Expectations

• Present the minilecture on "True Words." Discuss truth 2 in more detail by leading the group to complete ST 11. Note how Jesus' words emphasize God's original intention for marriage.

• Call on the two youth enlisted to report on their interviews as suggested in ST 12.

5. Revise Expectations

• Direct the group to complete ST 10. Ask for volunteers to share responses.

• Pray that each person will determine their expectations for marriage in relation to God's will and purposes.

• Assign chapter 3 for the next session.

Session 3
How Do I Communicate?

Session Goals: Youth will (1) experience the art of communication, (2) learn communication skills, and (3) apply communication techniques to specific situations.

AGENDA

1. Optical Illusion (15 Min.)
2. Word Association (15)
3. Listening Exercise (15)
4. Sharing Techniques (15)

Before the Session

☐ Study chapter 3 and complete the Stop and Think activities.

☐ On the chalkboard or large sheet of paper, draw the following diagram. Allow room to add the three diagrams shown in point 1 of "During The Session." Display the diagram on a focal wall.

☐ Make a list of words to use for a word-association activity. Choose words that relate to dating and marriage.

☐ Choose an object to describe and draw.

☐ Prepare a copy of the following group assignments.

Group 1. Read "Sharing What You Sense." Develop a two-sentence summary of this type of sharing. Complete ST 13.

Group 2. Read "Sharing What You Think." Develop a two-sentence summary of this type of sharing. Complete ST 14.

Group 3. Read "Sharing What You Feel." Develop a two-sentence summary of this type of sharing. Relate this type of sharing to the experience of Mark and Susan from chapter 2 in the section "False Idea 5: Everyone Knows What to Expect." Tell how this sharing would have helped Mark and Susan understand each other.

Group 4. Read "Sharing What You Intend." Develop a two-sentence summary of this type of sharing. Complete ST 16. Also tell why this kind of sharing is important in a dating or marriage relationship.

Group 5. Read "Sharing What You Do." Develop a two-sentence summary of this type of sharing. Complete ST 17.

During the Session

1. Optical Illusion

• Direct attention to the diagram on the focal wall. Ask, How many squares do you see in this diagram? After several have responded, state that, on first viewing, most people see 16 or 17 but that there actually are 25. Then draw the following three diagrams to show the 25 squares.

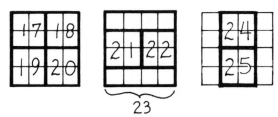

Note that this exercise reminds us that individuals see things differently. The difference in our perceptions makes some things difficult to understand while other things are easily apparent.

2. Word Association

• Have youth pair off with a person they do not know well. Tell the pairs to sit on the floor, back to back. Explain that they are to say aloud the first word that comes to mind when you give a cue word or phrase. When all the words have been called out, ask each pair to discuss the similarities and differences in their responses. When they have finished, ask, What does this reveal about the need to choose words carefully and to explain those that might cause a bad reaction?

3. Listening Exercise

• Distribute paper and pencils. Note that two other basic ingredients in communication are dialogue and listening skills. To illustrate the vital role these ingredients play in communication, lead the group in the following exercise. Then give these instructions: "I will draw a picture on my paper that you cannot see. I will describe to you exactly how to draw the same picture as I draw mine. You will have two restrictions, though. First, you cannot look at my paper. Second, you cannot talk from this point on. No matter how confused or frustrated you become, you must remain totally silent! It will not help to look at the person's drawing beside you, because that person may not hear correctly. Now that you have a totally positive idea of what is expected, I will tell you what to draw." (At this point, describe and draw your chosen object. Talk at a steady pace, using short and vague sentences.) When you are finished, hold up your paper for the group to see. Ask for volunteers to share their drawings. Then use the following questions to evaluate the experience: (1) How did you feel as I proceeded through my description—angry, frustrated, confused? (2) How did my lack of sensitivity to your plight make you feel? (3) Would it have helped for you to be able to question me as you went along? (4) Would the results have been better if my descriptions had been more detailed? (5) How does this exercise point out the necessity for careful description or definition and dialogue, if communication is to be effective?

4. Sharing Techniques

• Form small groups. Give each group a copy of the instructions prepared before the session. Call for reports.

• Pray that each person will grow in their ability to share.

• Assign chapter 4 for the next session. Encourage members to complete the ST activities.

Session 4
What Do I Believe and Live By?

Session Goals: Youth will (1) chart events in their lives, (2) experience the dynamics of cooperation, and (3) determine what marriage vows should include.

AGENDA

1. Make a Life Map (15 Min.)
2. Practice Cooperation (15)
3. Inventory Beliefs (15)
4. Examine Marriage Vows (15)

Before the Session
☐ Study chapter 4 and complete the Stop and Think activities.
☐ Secure a colored marker and a large sheet of paper for each member.
☐ Obtain from your pastor or from books several different wedding ceremonies and vows. Duplicate copies for small-group work. Also record the following questions on a sheet of paper (one set of questions for each group):

In what ways do these vows emphasize the priorities that have been mentioned?
Do they focus attention on the proper ideals for married life? Why or why not?
How do they tell the world which ideals the married couple stands for?
How would you change the vows?

☐ Enlist a youth to read Genesis 28:10-22.
☐ Study Ephesians 5:21-33. Be prepared to explain what these verses teach about mutual submission in marriage.
☐ Prepare copies of the following worksheet for all members. Insert numbers 1-8 under each "People" and "Objects" heading.

MAKE A LIST

DIRECTIONS: World War III has broken out; missiles are in flight and scheduled to hit this area in approximately 15 minutes. You are lucky. A space center in your town has a spaceship fueled and ready to depart for a new life on Mars. Your place is reserved, but you can take with you only eight other people and eight objects (such as a book, bicycle, and so forth). Consider objects and people in terms of these values: economic, sentimental, spiritual, social, occupational. You have only five minutes to accomplish this task. List below the persons and objects that you would take with you.

MY LIST

People   Objects

OUR LIST

People   Objects

During the Session

1. Make a Life Map

• Call on the youth enlisted to read Genesis 28:10-22. After the reading, interpret Jacob's need to put down a marker for a "holy place" in his life. State that we, like Jacob, need to put down markers for significant happenings in our lives. Explain that one way to do this is to engage in an exercise called "Mapping." Note that maps are guides that help us reach our destinations by way of reference points. Also, maps are items that we refer to again and again when we need to refresh our minds about directions.

Give each member a large sheet of paper and a marker. State that, in this activity, we will make a road map of our lives as we see them to this point. Direct members to draw a map depicting their life journey, complete with major cities (representing discoveries) and highways (representing changes in direction). The map will mark significant places in their lives. At each stop, members should be prepared to identify the place, the time in their life, why the event was important, what they learned there, and who helped them in their discovery. When they are finished, ask for volunteers to share their completed "map."

2. Practice Cooperation

• Distribute the worksheets prepared before the session. Allow time for members to list people and objects under "My List." Then form pairs and direct them to agree on a list of eight people and objects and to record that list under "Our List." After allowing five minutes to compile the list, call for reports.

Use the following questions to guide youth in evaluating this experience: What difficulties did you encounter in arriving at the joint list? Was it hard to give up something you considered essential? Why or why not? Who gave up the most, or was there mutual cooperation? How important do you think it is for couples to share the same feelings on important personal issues?

3. Inventory Beliefs

• Direct youth to complete ST 21. Suggest that they scan the section "What Is Most Important in Life?" as they determine answers. Allow 10 minutes for them to complete the activity. If some have not finished, suggest that they complete the activity after the session.

• Refer to ST 18 and 23. Ask for volunteers to name five beliefs that they cannot give up. After responses, ask, Why are these beliefs so important?

4. Examine Marriage Vows

• Form small groups. Distribute to the groups copies of the marriage vows and the questions (if possible, have a different set of vows for each group). State that marriage vows are a public way of saying to the world, to each other, and to God what a couple hopes to stand for together. Then direct the groups to answer the questions in relation to the marriage vows they have. After the groups report, read Ephesians 5:21 and explain the concept of mutual submission in marriage.

• Have members turn to ST 19. Read Genesis 2:24 and ask for volunteers to share what they wrote in ST 19.

Session 5
What Kind of Manager Am I?

Session Goals: Youth will (1) determine what is involved in being a manager, (2) develop work assignments in a family, and (3) agree on a budget.

AGENDA

1. Establish a Management Viewpoint (10 Min.)
2. Make Work Assignments (25)
3. Develop a Budget (25)

Before the Session

☐ Study chapter 5 and complete the Stop and Think activities.

☐ Enlist a youth to read Genesis 1:26-31. Enlist another youth to read the conversation between John and Sarah in the section "Establishing a Management Viewpoint."

☐ Design a worksheet to use in determining assignment of jobs in a household. Entitle the worksheet "Home Management." Under the title, record these directions: "Imagine that you are one of a couple, both of whom work outside the home. Consider the household jobs that need to be done. Check whether that responsibility should be assumed by husband or wife and when and how often the job needs to be done." Under these directions, line out three columns. Head column one "Job" and list these jobs chores under this title: cook breakfast, make bed, wash dishes, cook dinner, dust, vauum/sweep, clean bathroom, manage checkbook, pay bills, empty garbage, wash clothes, maintain car, shop for groceries. Head column two "Person Responsible." Under that title list "Husband" and "Wife" and subdivide this column into two. Head the third column "When? How often?" and "Other Comments." Duplicate copies of this worksheet for all members.

☐ Enlist two youth to interview an older couple (their parents, if possible) about how they developed a workable plan for managing their finances.

☐ Secure pocket calculators for group work.

During the Session

1. Establish a Management Viewpoint

• Write the word *manager* on the chalkboard. Ask for a volunteer to define the word. After responses, call on the youth enlisted to read Genesis 1:26-31. Ask, What do these verses say about being a manager? After responses, emphasize that God has given people the responsibility of being managers of His creation.

2. Make Work Assignments

• State that one aspect of being a good manager is helping things run smoothly in a family. Then form pairs and distribute the "Home Management" worksheets to the pairs. Tell them to use the worksheet to develop a fair division of household chores and responsibilities. Suggest that they add other chores they are aware of in their own families.

As the groups report, evaluate the job assignments to see what role stereotypes occurred and whether or not and why couples departed from the way things are done in their homes. Have them tell which issues were the hardest to work out.

3. Develop a Budget

• Call on the youth enlisted to read the conversation between John and Sarah. Ask, What problem does this couple need to work through?

• Have volunteers share what they wrote in ST 24.

• Form pairs and distribute calculators. Direct the pairs to complete ST 25 together. Also suggest that they resolve questions about how the money should be handled, such as whether they will have a joint checking account or two different accounts and which person will handle the checkbook. As leader, plan to be available to serve as financial consultant. Call for reports.

• Pray for wisdom in managing resources.

• Assign chapter 6 for the next session.

Session 6
How Do I Express My Sexuality?

Session Goals: Youth will (1) define sexuality, (2) determine responsibility in dating relationships, and (3) identify guidelines for roles in marriage.

AGENDA

1. Define Sexuality (15 Min.)
2. Identify Responsibility (25)
3. Consider Roles (20)

Before the Session
☐ Study chapter 6 and complete the Stop and Think activities.
☐ Display the collages created in session 2.
☐ Have available paper, pencils, extra study books, and Bibles.
☐ Make copies of the following case studies for group work.

Case study 1: Bob and Martha have been dating for the past two years and plan to marry six months from now. Their relationship has developed gradually to the point where they are faced with the question of sexual intercourse. Bob argues for intercourse on the grounds that it is a natural progression for their relationship and an expression of how they feel about each other. Martha disagrees, stating that, even though she is deeply in love with Bob, she feels that it is not right and that she would feel terribly guilty. Bob counters with the argument that intercourse is an expression of their love and is all right, because they will be married in just a few months anyway. Martha says she understands how he feels but that she can't go through with it, and she plans to talk to a counselor to help her understand her feelings. Bob blows up, claiming that her actions are a breach of trust in the relationship. He warns that, if she doesn't come around to his point of view, they obviously don't have the trust necessary to get married. What should Martha do?

Case study 2: A few months ago, Mary moved to Bridge City from a smaller town where she was extremely popular and well-liked. Since moving to Bridge City, she has had a difficult time finding her place and crowd. After some time, Fred in her English class, asks her to a Friday-night party. He explains that they will triple-date in his dad's van with two couples from school. Mary gladly accepts, because, not only is Fred good-looking and friendly, but it is her chance to get into the Bridge City social scene. On Friday, when Fred arrives for the date, Mary is pleased at the favorable impression he gives her parents. Once inside the van, she is further pleased to discover that the other two couples are part of what she considers the popular crowd of Bridge City. At the party Mary feels at home, enjoying the friendly and congenial atmosphere. But, after only an hour or so, Fred says that the rest of the group is ready to go. Mary agrees, even though she is disappointed. The last thing in the world she wants to do is create a scene. After leaving the party, the group drives around for a while, finally ending up at the lake. Fred parks the van at a secluded spot, and the other two couples begin to engage in heavy petting. Fred nervously puts his arm around Mary and draws her close to him with the intention of pursuing the same kind of activity. While Mary is not opposed to kissing on the first date, she feels rather uncomfortable about what is happening. Fred senses her uneasiness and asks, "You're not one of those small-town prudes, are you? Mary is hurt and confused. What should she do?

During the Session

1. Define Sexuality

• Direct attention to the collages created in session 2. Ask, How does the media affect our understanding of maleness and femaleness? After responses, form small groups of only male and female. Direct the girls to read the section "Being Male" and the boys to read the section "Being Female." Ask the girls to complete this sentence: "Being male means. . . ." Ask the boys to complete this sentence: "Being female means. . . ." As the groups report, allow time for those of the opposite sex to respond to the conclusions.

• Guide members in completing ST 28. Lead the group to agree on a definition of *sexuality*. Record the definition on the chalkboard.

2. Identify Responsibility

• Give the same small groups one of the case studies. If your group is large, you could give the same case study to more than one group. Direct them to carefully read the case study and determine answers to the question at the end. Call for reports.

• Guide members in completing and discussing Stop and Think activities 30 and 31. Expand the discussion with these questions: How big a part does sex play in dating? Who makes the decisions about the way dating time is spent? How have double standards for male and female sexual behavior been implied in our culture? How does one say no and at what point? What guidelines can Christians establish for sex and dating?

3. Consider Roles

• Form pairs. Direct them to complete ST 29, based on the discussion during this session. Call for volunteers to share answers.

• Pray that members will let Christian standards determine their dating activities.

• Assign chapter 7 for the next session. Again, encourage members to complete the Stop and Think activities.

Session 7
What Am I to Do? and You?

Session Goals: Youth will (1) explain the difference between approaching life from a technique viewpoint and a purpose viewpoint, (2) state why a Christian should marry a person who feels that God directs one's life, (3) tell how gift discovery is related to selecting a vocation, and (4) determine ways for a couple to work through potential problems about the selection of a vocation.

AGENDA

1. Express a Philosophy of Life (15 Min.)
2. Identify What God Wants (15)
3. Discover Gifts (15)
4. Solve Potential Problems (15)

Before the Session

☐ Study chapter 7 and complete the Stop and Think activities.

☐ Study Matthew 25:19-27. Be prepared to explain what these verses teach about discovering and using God's gifts to us. Plan to refer to the section "Discovering and Using Gifts and Abilities" as you explain the verses.

☐ Enlist a youth to be prepared to read Matthew 25:19-27.

☐ Have available paper, pencils, extra study books, and extra Bibles.

☐ Enlist four youth to role play the following situations. Give them copies of the descriptions well in advance of the session.

Role play 1: Jan, who plans to pursue a career, and Thomas, who feels called to a church-related vocation, are trying to determine how they both can work toward their goals after they get married. Jan wants to move up the management ladder. Thomas wants to be free to move from one church to another as the Lord directs. Role play a conversation in which they suggest ways to help each other work toward their goals.

Role play 2: Jim works for a company that has offices all over the world. In all probability, he will have to move to a new location from time to time to advance in the company. Margaret has lived in one place all her life and likes it. She loves Jim but dreads the possibility of moving away from her hometown. Role play a conversation in which they suggest ways to work through their differences.

During the Session

1. Express a Philosophy of Life

• As members arrive, direct them to complete ST 33. For ideas, suggest that they scan the first two sections in the chapter: "Approaching the Adventure" and "Considering Technique vs. Purpose." Ask for volunteers to share what they wrote. Call attention to specific examples from the chapter, such as the story about the rich young ruler in Mark 10:17-22. Also note contemporary ways people live by technique rather than purpose.

To further expand the discussion of technique and purpose, write this statement on the chalkboard: "You can live life, or you can let life live you." Ask, How does that statement describe the difference between living by purpose and living by technique? After responses, state that Christians should be guided by God's purposes for their lives as they choose a vocation. To emphasize this point, read the following statement from the chapter: "Discover the purpose for your life and then live out that purpose wherever and whatever your job may be."

2. Identify What God Wants

• Have members complete the first activity in ST 34. Ask volunteers to share what they found. Record statements on the chalkboard. If no one mentions the following statement, add it to the list: "God's will is that we be the best persons we can be." If the statement is named, circle it. Ask, Why is it important that a Christian marry someone who feels that God directs his or her life? Allow time for several to respond.

• Form pairs. Direct them to complete the other activities in ST 34 individually and then share what they wrote with each other.

3. Discover Gifts

• Call on the youth enlisted to read Matthew 25:19-27. Then give a minilecture on the meaning of these verses as they relate to discovering and using God's gifts to us (refer to the section "Discovering and Using Gifts and Abilities").

• Guide members in completing ST 35. Have several volunteers share what they wrote.

4. Solve Potential Problems

• Call on the persons enlisted to present the role plays. After each role play, use these questions to guide the group in evaluating the way the couples resolved their problems: Do you agree with the way the couple solved the problem? Why or why not? Do you think they communicated their feelings and goals well? Why or why not? Would you have solved the problem differently? If so, how?

• Guide the group in completing ST 36. Ask for volunteers to share responses.

• Pray for wisdom in selecting a vocation.

• Assign chapter 8 for the next session. Encourage members to complete the Stop and Think activities.

Session 8
What Is My Family Like?
What Will My New Family Be?

Session Goals: Youth will (1) state reasons marriage should be for adults, (2) identify ways a person's present family influences a future family, and (3) determine actions to take to resolve certain issues that affect a marriage relationship.

AGENDA

1. Determine Who Should Marry (10 Min.)
2. Anticipate a New Family (15)
3. Resolve Issues (35)

Before the Session
☐ Study chapter 8 and complete the Stop and Think activities.
☐ Duplicate for all members copies of the worksheet on page 142.
☐ Enlist two youth to be prepared to report on ST 38. Provide resources for them to use.
☐ Enlist a youth to interview two couples, using the questions in ST 40.
☐ Have available paper, pencils, extra study books, and Bibles.

During the Session
1. Determine Who Should Marry
• Ask, Who should get married? After responses, guide members in answering the second question in ST 37.
2. Anticipate a New Family
• Distribute the worksheets (p. 142). When members finish, ask for volunteers to respond to these questions: What emotions developed as you completed the worksheet? How do you think your present family will affect the way you do things in your future family? What will you try to do the same? What will you change? After several have responded, state that the ques-

tions on the worksheet were designed to evaluate their relationship to their present family as they anticipate being part of a new family. Suggest they keep the worksheet for future reference.

3. Resolve Issues

• Direct the group to scan chapter 8 and underline issues or new experiences that affect marriage relationships. Ask for volunteers to tell what they underlined. List responses on the chalkboard. Items should include the following: separation from family of origin, meeting future in-laws, transferring allegiance to mate, accepting and loving in-laws, becoming a parent.

• Form groups. Assign one of the following issues to each group (if your group is small, assign more than one issue to a group). Tell the groups to read the section that corresponds to their assignment as outlined below. They should then list the main points brought out in that section about how to resolve the issue. Make sure the persons enlisted to report on ST 38 are in the group assigned "Shifting Loyalties." Direct the group assigned the subject of meeting in-laws to complete ST 39. Direct the group assigned the subject of parenting to complete ST 41. Plan to call for reports on these activities as the groups report.

(1) Separation from family of origin—"Families and Independence"
(2) Transferring allegiance to mate—"Shifting Loyalties"
(3) Meeting future in-laws—"Meeting Prospective In-laws"
(4) Accepting and loving in-laws—"Loving In-laws"
(5) Becoming a parent—"Planning a Family"

As the groups report, fill in details from the study material as necessary. Allow time for members to respond to the suggested dialog in ST 39 and the answers for ST 41.

• Call on the person enlisted to interview two couples with the questions in ST 40. Allow time for members to respond to the report, based on the discussion during this session.

• Pray for guidance in choosing a marriage partner.

A FAMILY INVENTORY

1. Which person in your family takes major responsibility in the following areas?

a. Discipline _____

b. Finances _____

c. Starting communication _____

d. Planning recreation _____

e. Religious activities _____

f. Sharing love _____

g. Handling crisis situations _____

2. What activities does your family participate in together? For example, do you all eat together or do schedules of family members require a more flexible arrangement?

_____

3. If your family could be described as revolving around one person's personality, who would it be and why?

_____

4. How does your family affect what you envision for your future family? What do you appreciate most about your family? Least?

_____

5. What characteristics would you like for your spouse's family to have?

_____

6. What family would you like yours to be like, other than your own? Why?

_____

The Church Study Course

The Church Study Course is a Southern Baptist education system designed to support the training efforts of local churches. It provides courses, recognition, record keeping, and regular reports for some 20,000 participating churches. This education system is characterized by short courses ranging from 21/2 to 10 hours in length. They may be studied individually or in groups. With more than 600 courses in 24 subject areas, it offers 130 diploma plans in all areas of church leadership and Christian growth.

Complete details about the Church Study Course system, courses available, and diplomas offered may be found in a current copy of the *Church Study Course Catalog.* The Church Study Course system is jointly sponsored by many agencies within the Southern Baptist Convention.

How to Request Credit for This Course

This book is the text for course number 17-043 in the subject area: "The Christian Family." The course is designed for 8 hours of group study. Credit for this course may be obtained in two ways:

1. Read the book and attend class sessions. (If you are absent from one or more sessions, complete the "Stop and Think" activities for the material missed.)

2. Read the book and complete the "Stop and Think" activities. (Written work should be submitted to an appropriate church leader.)

A request for credit may be made on Form 725 "Church Study Course Enrollment/Credit Request" and sent to the Awards Office, Sunday School Board, 127 Ninth Avenue, North, Nashville, Tennessee 37234. The form on the following page may be used to request credit. Enrollment in a diploma plan may also be made on Form 725. Within three months of your completion of a course, confirmation of your credit will be sent to your church. A copy of your complete transcript will be sent to your church annually during the July–September quarter, if you have completed a course during the previous 12 months.

CHURCH STUDY COURSE
ENROLLMENT/CREDIT REQUEST
FORM - 725 (Rev. 1-89)

MAIL THIS REQUEST TO →

CHURCH STUDY COURSE AWARDS OFFICE
BAPTIST SUNDAY SCHOOL BOARD
127 NINTH AVENUE, NORTH
NASHVILLE, TENNESSEE 37234

Is this the first course taken since 1983? ☐ YES If yes, or not sure complete all of Section 1. ☐ NO If no, complete only bold boxes in Section 1.

SECTION 1 - STUDENT I.D.

STUDENT

Social Security Number | Personal CSC Number* →

☐ Mr. ☐ Miss
☐ Mrs.

DATE OF BIRTH — Month | Day | Year

Name (First, MI, Last)

Street, Route, or P.O. Box

City, State | Zip Code

CHURCH

Church Name

Mailing Address

City, State | Zip Code

SECTION 2 - CHANGE REQUEST ONLY (Current inf. in Section1)

☐ Former Name

☐ Former Address | Zip Code

☐ Former Church | Zip Code

SECTION 3 - COURSE CREDIT REQUEST

Course No.	Title (use exact title)
1. 17-043	Before you Marry
2.	
3.	
4.	
5.	
6.	

SECTION 4 - DIPLOMA ENROLLMENT

Enter exact diploma title from current Church Study Course catalog. Indicate diploma age group if appropriate. Do not enroll again with each course. When all requirements have been met, the diploma will be mailed to your church. Enrollment in Christian Development Diplomas is automatic. No charge will be made for enrollment or diplomas.

Title of Diploma	Age group or area
Title of Diploma	Age group or area
Signature of Pastor, Teacher, or Other Church Leader	Date

*CSC # not required for new students. Others please give CSC # when using SS # for the first time. Then, only one ID # is required.